The Yoga Stripper

A Las Vegas Memoir of Sex, Drugs, and Namaste

Laila Lucent

ISBN: 1482000091
ISBN-13: 978-1482000092

For Adderall, Alcohol, and Rockstar Energy Drink
Without all of you in my life, truly, none of this would
have been possible.

And for
Buffy the Vampire Slayer

Table of Contents

"You have to laugh at the things that hurt you just to keep yourself in balance, just to keep the world from running you plumb crazy... You can't really be strong until you can see a funny side to things."

Kesey, *One Flew Over the Cuckoo's Nest*

"Most virtue is a demand for greater seduction."

Natalie Barney

AN INTRODUCTION

"Our stripper is broken. We need a new stripper!"

As though someone had flipped a switch on a mechanical doll, the blonde stripper who just moments ago had been drinking and talking is slumped over, unconscious. We all laugh. The billionaire in my group leaves to find a bouncer.

It's 6 a.m. on Easter Sunday. I'm topless in the VIP section of the Spearmint Rhino with a group of Europeans: a billionaire, a DJ, an ex-stripper turned gynecologist, and now, a passed out stripper. I can't think of a better way to celebrate the rebirth of Jesus Christ.

A bouncer comes into the room and carries the blonde away. Now, I'm the entertainment for the whole group.

"I told the bouncer the stripper passed out," the billionaire says. "He asked if we wanted a refund, and I said *no*. We were just worried about her safety. Also, I tipped him really well so we can do whatever we want now."

"I want to dance for you," the gynecologist says to me. This is how I used to dance when I worked at the Spearmint Rhino in London." I sit topless as this hot smart girl shakes her ass in my face. *I love my job, right now.*

11

"I was thinking," the billionaire says to me, "How about we move this party to a hotel room? We'll pay you a lot of money."

"No!" the DJ says, "She's not like that. I don't want you to convince her to do anything. She's a writer. She's not going to be stripping for long… she's a writer." *Aw, my white knight is defending my honor.* What he said is true. I am a writer, and I won't be doing this for long – hopefully. However, that the DJ believes anything I've told him tonight in order to get his money is adorable. I've been known to lie. A lot. About everything.

"The DJ is one of the coolest guys I've been with in the VIP," I tell the ex-stripper when she sits back down beside me. "I think he really likes me."

"Yeah, he's a good guy," she says. "I'm a friend of his wife. We're all in Vegas together this weekend. She's asleep." *Ah, strip club romance.*

"We need to figure out what to tell my fiancé and your wife about where we've been all night," the billionaire says. "Maybe we can say we've been gambling."

When they leave at 9 a.m., I get paid $1300. If you want to hang out with me for the night, then you'll need a lot of money and be able to come up with a good lie about what you've been doing. After all, I'm a Las Vegas stripper.

LET ME KNOW IF YOU FIGURE IT OUT

"What are *you* doing *here*?"

"Stripping for money. What are you doing here?"

"Umm… I'm… giving you money to strip?"

"Sounds good to me! Let's get a dance."

"Okay!"

During my two years as a Las Vegas stripper, I had this conversation thousands of times.

The underlying subtext of this conversation was:

"Why are you stripping? You're such a clean, smart, nice girl. You could be a reporter for Fox News, or do PR for Middle Eastern dictators, or design the green labels for plastic water bottles, you know, something respectable."

"I'm sorry you disapprove, random guy I'm trying to get money from at a strip club. Men pay me to dance topless, I understand what I'm doing, and I think it's great! I have money, free time, and I get to travel. You're only meeting me because,

13

apparently, you're just as morally bankrupt as you're implying I am."

"You're right! I'm being a hypocritical dickhead. I would love to see your breasts for money. I didn't mean to imply anything different. I love boobs, and yours are real which is wonderful."

"I accept your apology. Now give me money, and I'll take off my bra."

"Okay!"

I can have entire strip club conversations without paying any attention to what I'm saying. One time, I approached a man for a dance. I walked up, put my arms around his neck, made my pupils dilate on cue (oh yeah, girl has got skills), and asked him his name.

"You've got to be joking," he looked at me and said. "I just got a dance from you 20 minutes ago. Don't you remember?"

Oops, sorry, I guess I'm the dickhead.

**

Obviously, this was not ladylike behavior.

But I was straight out of college, newly heartbroken, completely disillusioned, and secretly hoping the world would end in 2012, and I'd be off the hook for figuring out the rest of my life. I was shameless and, more importantly, I was damn good at sales.

If you're a man, and you think you've got the best game, the ladies fall at your feet, and you can make anybody do anything for you at anytime… sit down, shut up, and get out a pen and paper. You're going to want to take notes.

The Spearmint Rhino strippers in Las Vegas have game that is world-renowned. If your husband or boyfriend was in Las Vegas between 2010 and 2012, there's a good chance I sat on his lap, raised my left leg straight up by my head, "giggle-bounced," and cooed in his ear, "I'm a yoga instructor."

"Whoa, calm down, lady! I would have danced for you too if you'd been there. Let's not get possessive. I'm not trying to take your man. I don't want him. I want the contents of his wallet."

"I'm sorry, ma'am! I swear it meant nothing to either of us. It's just that men have these uncontrollable hormones that run amok, and I have bills to pay and my mouth to keep fed with organic vegetables. Are you aware there's a recession out there? Personally, I blame the economy. Chill out. Don't hit me. I bruise easily."

You haven't seen game until you've gone into the Spearmint Rhino on a Saturday night at 2:30 a.m. and seen hundreds of shockingly beautiful women strutting around, licking their lips, and eyeing their prey. The Rhino's a trip - let me tell you. You're guaranteed to leave broke but with a huge smile on your face.

This memoir is one of those reverse fairy tales where the wicked stepmothers and ugly stepsisters of the world finally get the chance to tell their side of the story. I can't tell you why other girls make the choice to strip, other than the money, and I understand a lot of it is unhealthy, and I understand I may be the exception and not the rule, but this isn't a story about the rule. There's enough written about that side of things. I want to tell my side.

There are happy, healthy, well-adjusted strippers out there; mucking up the status quo. You can find them: speaking Spanish during their summers in Spain, putting themselves through graduate school, working towards their pilot licenses, killing it on stage in your weekly improv comedy classes, and backpacking with their adoring husbands across Europe. Some of the most exceptional women I've met in my life, I met stripping at the

15

Spearmint Rhino. This book is for them, because I want the world to know they exist.

This is the story about my quarter-life crisis on the Las Vegas strip, and it's one of my very favorite stories – if only because *The Yoga Stripper* is "my story." Try to be kind.

"Let him who is without sin among you be the first to throw a stone at her."

Moralizing isn't attractive. In fact, it's boring - which is the opposite of attractive. Everyone wants to be seductive and desirable, whether you're loose enough to admit it to yourself or not.

"It is absurd to divide people into good and bad. People are either charming or tedious," Oscar Wilde explained. Which are you?

HOW THE HELL DID I END UP HERE?

How did a nice, college-educated, Midwestern, country girl, who loves her family more than anything else, end up a deviant Las Vegas stripper? Here are my three main reasons (There are many more, including the undisputed fact that boobies are awesome, but these are the main ones):

Philosopher Kings

My college boyfriend, Luke, and I were philosophers. Well, Luke was a philosopher, and I was a totally smitten little girl. Wow, how I loved that man! Feeling something so profoundly intensely wonderful as that kind of love makes a person glad to be alive. We'd take psychedelics and question the nature of reality. We'd listen to Pink Floyd and quote Socrates to one another.

"A wise man knows he knows nothing." Luke and I concluded that what we're conditioned to see isn't the only truth to everything going on. We questioned right and wrong, good and bad, and we asked Why of everything, chasing it down the rabbit hole, until there was no Why left to ask. Turns out, there is no good and bad, only "good for something" or "bad for something." If you want to convince me that stripping is bad, I'd welcome that conversation, and you better come prepared for a healthy debate.

Freedom's Just Another Word For Nothing Left to Lose

A few months before we met, during our freshman year of college, Luke became friends with a girl named Tiffany. Tiffany was a gorgeous, alpha sorority blonde, and she could easily intimidate with her calculated indifference.

Senior year of college, Tiffany lost her keys at a Halloween party, and a room of slutty pirates and Little Miss Muffets ran around asking the guests, "Have you seen Tiffany's keys? She's lost her keys."

Because she was always around, Tiffany and I became friends. Of course, we were more competitors than real friends, but a little competition is good for the heart, and we were well matched. My boyfriend was always a bit obsessed with Tiffany, and that meant I was always *very* obsessed with her. We were the type of friends women make when they feel threatened.

"Oh, you're Laila? Well aren't you beautiful. My boyfriend keeps talking about how great your yoga classes are! We should be best friends, tell each other all of our secrets, and never be apart, because I love you!" Unfortunately, jealousy and insecurity are not a solid foundation for friendship.

Honestly, I loved Tiffany. Although she was far from being stable or kind, she was really interesting. She had a hookah with pillows all around it in her room that she'd brought back from a summer abroad in India. She studied international business and spoke really terrible Spanish. She had a record player and doodled pictures of Jim Morrison. She was really brave and shameless, and a hell of a lot of fun. I have a lot of great memories starring her. Tiffany would always be the star of any situation, or she'd be willing to die trying. It's too bad about everything that happened, because she's one of my favorite characters.

While I'd been with Luke for four years, Tiffany didn't care about, or wasn't capable of, a real relationship. Tiffany had a man fly her to Turkey for a vacation. She joked about having sex with a man in exchange for a weekend at a lake resort. She kissed one man to make another jealous. Senior year, she even went on a threesome spree. Yes, I just wrote *threesome spree*. She was as charming as she was pathological. She didn't give a damn, and I saw the power that flaunting the rules gave her. I saw the way men, including my boyfriend, responded to Tiffany, and I envied her fearlessness and independence.

Finally, senior year, Tiffany lived in the same house as five guys, across the hall from my boyfriend. The night before Tiffany moved away to her new job in Cleveland, Luke and I had just gone to sleep, when we heard her come home drunk. She was in the hallway, outside of Luke's room, laughing with a sorority friend.

"Luke! Luke, come out here!" Tiffany yelled. At first, we kept sleeping, but she yelled again.

"Luke! Come on! Come out here!"

"This is going to be crazy," Luke said as he sighed, pulled on pants, and left the room.

I fell back asleep, and I didn't wake up again until Luke returned and tried to climb back over me into bed.

"Baby, where were you?" I asked, half asleep.

"I, uh, well, I…" Luke stammered.

"What? Where were you?" I repeated.

"I can't lie to you, baby. I'm so sorry! I just had a threesome with Tiffany and Jennifer across the hall!" Luke said, freaking out, as he curled into a fetal position beside me on the bed. "I'm so sorry, baby!"

Once I was awake enough to understand what he'd said, I got out of bed and gathered my clothes to the pathetic sounds of,

"I'm so sorry baby. I can't even look at you. I'm so ashamed of myself. I'm so sorry."

You get to pick one or the other, damn it! Either have the threesome and don't tell me, or don't have the threesome! These are the two logical choices. This was not logical. This was insanity. This insanity, this unanswerable Why, played on repeat across my brain. I didn't know how to silence the screaming. Luke and Tiffany would come nightly to see me in my dreams. They'd tell me how in love they were, and how I'd been in their way for four years. I lay comatose on my bed for months, unable to move or feel.

I didn't know what to do without Luke, he'd been my best friend, and I didn't give a damn about any other man. I didn't believe in this love bullshit anymore; look what it had gotten me after all. The last thing I wanted was a man to love me forever. I no longer respected men, and I didn't care if they respected me. Seriously, fuck your love; give me your money.

Next, my friend Seth got the ax from his long-term girlfriend too.

"I'm moving to Vegas, and you should come live with me," Seth said to me one day, between bong rips. "Vegas will piss off both of our exes, and we'll have fun living together." Through the cloud of THC infused smoke permeating my head, Seth made a lot of sense. I had no job prospects in Ohio, I knew I wanted to head out West to seek my fortune, and without a man to call my own, I had no reason left to stick around.

What better place to indulge my inner demons than in the overwhelming darkness obscured beneath the neon of the Sin City night?

A few months later, all of my possessions were packed up in my beat-up 2003 Toyota Corolla, and I was driving solo cross-country to my new desert home.

Stripping = Topless Promotional Modeling

The original plan was to do promotions in Vegas while I worked on my writing and lived as though I was on vacation for a year or two. For the last three years of college, I'd picked up extra cash doing promotional modeling for everyone from Capri Sun to Corvette Racing. Vegas, being the home of endless conventions, seemed the perfect place to buy myself some time by living off of my looks. A person should play to their strengths, and with a bachelor's degree in strategic communication and no "real world" experience; I knew my biggest strengths were my A+ bullshitting skills and a great rack.

I'd spent three years being objectified by men for $15 to $20 an hour while telling them to drink alcohol or listen to sports radio.

"Are you completely shaven down there?" they'd ask me after I'd handed them a free shot at a bar.

"You naughty boy! I'm not going to tell you that!" Bullshit personified with a brain dead giggle-bounce is what they were paying me to do, and I understood that just fine.

In a college business course, they taught us to, if possible, cut out the middleman – go straight from wholesale to buyer. I'd spent three years selling tits and ass under the guise of product promotion. Why not cut out the beer companies' profits and make $100 an hour instead of $15? And, as an added bonus, I knew when my now ex-boyfriend discovered my new occupation, he'd be destroyed. I smiled at the thought. It felt good to smile again.

And thus I found myself, at twenty-two, approaching the big burly bouncers guarding the back entrance of The Spearmint Rhino in Las Vegas to find out what to bring for my audition later that night.

WHAT'S THE INTERVIEW PROCESS LIKE FOR THIS POSITION?

The bouncers stared at me as I approached the back door of the Spearmint Rhino. In Ohio, all of the job interviews I'd gone on required knee-length skirts and shirts that would make me look classy, smart, and responsible - not like the sexual harassment liability I actually was. Wearing heels, a pencil skirt, and a low cut shirt, it was obvious I didn't belong there. I pushed down the nerves and walked up to the men in black.

"Hi, I'm here looking for a job?"

The two bouncers behind the desk smirked at me.

"What kind of job do you want to get here?" one of them asked incredulously.

"Dancer." It was true. I did want to be a dancer - not a waitress, or hostess, or something tamer. I wanted to be on par with the wildest girls in Vegas; no one was going to out-crazy me. I was unstable, damn it, and someone needed to pay me for how irresponsible I was planning on being.

"Dancer? We don't have any dancers working here," the bouncers could smell my fear. I was too afraid to even say the *word* "stripper," and they weren't going to let me get away with the euphemism. I wasn't a ballerina; I was a hustler who had zero qualms about taking off my clothes for money. There is, at least, a slight difference.

A tattooed blonde in lingerie walked through the back room, smiled warmly at the bouncers, and stood holding onto the front of a large fan.

"I just got off of stage. It's hot up there!" She laughed and continued into the locker room.

Oh man, deep breathes. Go away from fear, I coached myself. *Fear is the path to the dark side.* If you can't trust Yoda, then there's no one you can trust for sound advice.

"Do you have any dancing experience?"

"Not professionally." *I'm hip, I'm cool, and I'm where I belong - or not. Wow, do these guys look amused.*

"Not professionally? What does that mean?"

"I haven't danced for money before."

"So you give it up for free then?"

"I guess. I've danced for my ex-boyfriend before." Innocence gets no respect at the Rhino.

"What's a sweet young thing like you want to work here for?"

"The money."

"Hey, that's why I work here."

"We have so much in common."

The bouncers told me to come back at nine that night with a two-piece outfit and heels. Oh yeah, baby, the adrenaline rush! Gambling, stripping, teetering on the brink of destruction – I'm a thrill junkie.

That afternoon, I felt as though I was getting ready for the first day of school.

What are all the other kids going to be wearing? I want them to like me, and I want them to think I'm cool.

I didn't have much money; I'd driven cross-country with less than $2,000 in my bank account, but fancy lingerie and glitter heels were now tax-deductible investments. I went shopping and spent the day restless in anticipation.

SIZE MATTERS – THE SPEARMINT RHINO IS HUGE

The Spearmint Rhino is not what you're thinking. When most people picture a strip club, they imagine 15 girls who make their money by dancing on the stage. In the Rhino, with 20,000 square feet, dancing on the stage was an unwelcome interruption, because the real money was out on the floor. There were hundreds of women working every weekend. I almost never recognized anyone, and it took over a year working at the Rhino for anyone to recognize me.

The best part of the job was that I could work whenever I wanted. I hear some strip clubs around the country have schedules, but at the Rhino, we were free to come and go as we pleased. No one cared if I came into the Rhino or not. Once I was at the Rhino, no one cared if I worked or not. I could work every night or no nights. I could hustle hard all night, or I could sit in the back in sweatpants reading Las Vegas Weekly magazine. I could leave for a month-long vacation on a whim. I could choose to make money or not to make money. Strippers work for tips, and this weeded out the inarticulate and the ugly. If no one wanted dances from you, then you wouldn't make any money, and you wouldn't bother stripping for long.

Sexuality can be simplified to a science, and the women inside the Rhino manufactured themselves as sex personified. Every trick to enhance natural beauty was used and abused, and once the darkness hid the flaws, everyone looked perfect. Aspiring actresses made the weekly trip from LA, to make the money for their next facial, on their quest to become famous starlets. Men asked if I knew the other girls, but the Rhino was an endless carousel of new faces, and I only recognized a handful of them.

The Rhino was crowded. Some nights, the hundreds of lockers in the locker room would be full, and girls would need to throw their designer bags in a big pile in the locker room for the house mom to protect for the night.

Lap dances on the crowded floor cost $20, but the real money was made in the VIP, which ranged in price from $100 for three songs to $775 for a curtained-off hour.

What can you do more in the VIP than out on the floor? Why should a man pay all that money for VIP time with a stripper?

Well, I'm on Team Stripper, not Team Tourist; all I can tell you about VIP time is that, "No matter what a stripper tells you, there's no sex in the Champagne Room," or any other VIP room for that matter. Other than no sex, come on into The Spearmint Rhino next time you're in Vegas and see what the strippers tell you can happen in the VIP. I hear a lot of the girls have pretty wild sales pitches.

I will say, "If you do have the money, then the VIP room is definitely worth your time. You only live once, after all. Look into my startlingly blue eyes; look how honest they are. You can trust me... Great! Now, give a stripper all of your money."

At any time, the VIP rooms could easily accommodate hundreds of people. Yet, despite the large supply of VIP seating, there was usually still a line to get in one, and after a certain hour, Celebrity, the most expensive room, was impossible to use. When a big convention was in town, I'd be forced to make all of my money by giving $20 lap dances on the floor, because the line to get into one of the VIP rooms could be over an hour. There are very few things more awkward than having to make chitchat with a horny man waiting in line for the VIP room.

"I know you're about to give me $200 for half an hour with my breasts, but first, I'd love for you to tell me about your flight into Vegas. Was there turbulence?"

Okay, the Rhino is a crazy, high energy, sexually charged, extravagant, mad place to work, and that's the way I like it. Now, let's get on with the story about the time I was a stripper in Las Vegas.

MAKE IT RAIN, TRICK

Wearing heels and lingerie, I took my place next to the other stripper-hopefuls waiting to audition. I looked at a sign on the wall that explained the legal definition of prostitution: "Agreeing to sexually arouse for money." Coincidentally, this is the exact description of the job I was trying to get.

A line of jaded strippers waiting to check-in for work stretched out the door. Wearing unflattering sweatpants and T-shirts, most of them already looked exhausted by the mere thought of all the bullshit they were about to dish out and put up with that night. Underneath their masks of makeup, fake eyelashes, fake breasts, fake lips, dyed blonde hair and extensions, I watched beautiful aging faces melt in the light. Makeup caked into creased skin. Chanel, Prada, and Louis Vuitton purses rested on each and every shoulder. What used to symbolize status now symbolized occupation.

A lovely black girl stood nervously next to me, clad in lingerie.

"Have you danced before?" I asked her.

"No… I haven't. Some friends of mine work here, and they convinced me to come in and try out. They said working here is fun, and I can make over a thousand dollars in a night. I don't know why I'm here. This isn't like me."

Holy shit, in Vegas, girls peer pressure their friends into stripping? This place is so much fun! I knew I was going to like working here.

"Yeah, this is my first time too," I said.

"I don't know why I'm even here... I'm not really like this. I work in retail, you know? I don't know if I can do this. They just said it's a lot of money." I hoped this girl didn't start crying; I'd feel uncomfortable.

What's the audition going to be like? I worried. *Will I have to pass a series of increasingly difficult and degrading tests? Will the manager leer at me and suggest I come back to his place for the real audition? Will I be asked to strip naked and dance in front of a terrifying panel of bouncer judges?*

The night manager Jim, his face always blank and hard, walked up to the line of girls. *What terrible test would I have to pass?*

"For your audition," he said, "You're going to walk by me, turn around, and walk back." *Oh, well, that was a bit anticlimactic.*

Jim pointed at the first girl, and she walked. She was short and chubby, and she was told that she could only come to work in the early afternoon. If you don't look like you walked off the pages of *Maxim*, then you're not walking into the Rhino at night.

The next girl walked. She had slim runners legs, round and full natural breasts, no butt, and a cute face. She was put on the 2:30 a.m. shift.

"Keep this card with you," a bouncer told her. "Most girls are 3 a.m. The card lets us know you're allowed coming in at 2:30 a.m." This time of night is when all of the horny men who didn't pick up girls at the clubs on the strip are let out into the Vegas night; it's prime moneymaking time at the strip clubs. The late night shift is really a great shift to work, other than that the earliest

29

you can leave is 7:00 a.m., and that's if the manager is feeling generous.

When I opted to work the 2:30 a.m. shift, I'd walk out into the morning sun, shield my eyes, and sit with the other girls in workout wear waiting for the mandatory safety valet to retrieve my car. Alarm clocks set to wake me at 1:00 a.m. and the bizarre nature of night becoming daytime while I scrambled for hundreds in the pitch darkness gave stripping a dream-like quality.

"Is this real life?"

"No, this is Las Vegas."

I was up. I walked past Jim. I walked back over to him. I'm pretty much the walking champion of the world.

I was given a card for 7 p.m., one of the best work shifts but not the *very best* work shift. The best work shift was 9 p.m. and was filled with physically perfect silicone blondes and older strippers who'd been grandfathered in. I'd heard talk of 11 p.m. shift girls, but they were mythical creatures I suspected didn't truly exist. I never met any of them at least. Although, I did meet several girls who claimed to be allowed to come in at whatever time they wanted.

Girls who would have easily been given any shift at any other club in Las Vegas would be relegated to the 2:30 am shift at the Rhino for being a bit too heavy, having too little of an ass, too small of a chest, too broken out of a face, too brown of hair, or any other slight defect in physicality.

This pressure to be physically perfect caused all of us to act crazy. There were girls who could only come in during the day; girls who had to leave by 11 p.m.; girls Jim, the night manager, would tell, usually when they looked too happy and full of life, that he didn't know why he put them on such an early shift. One night, I saw a girl crying. She'd had liposuction because, months before, Jim had told her she was too heavy for the 9 p.m. shift. She'd auditioned again post-surgery, and she still didn't make the cut. She'd spent thousands of dollars to improve her appearance in order to make more money, and she was left on 3 a.m. shift and told she still wasn't beautiful enough. It was merciless.

Personally, I chose to obsess over my butt. Naturally I don't have one, and only through the power of yoga and spin class, can I make my butt into somewhat of a respectable shape. Truly, my butt is not such a bad butt. Sometimes, I've even been complimented, but I never believe anyone. Instead, I chalk their kind words off to flattery. My butt is really not so awful. If I was in a room of randomly selected people, my butt would surely break the top ten percent, perhaps even five percent. But in a room of women paid to play largely on their curves, I felt my butt was inadequate. My butt could definitely have stood to be perkier, larger, and rounder. Sometimes, when I was dancing on one of the side stages, I'd see my disembodied butt in the mirror. I'd try to decide how I would feel about its shape and size if it wasn't attached to me. I was sure if only I could make my butt perfect, I would be given the coveted 9 p.m. shift. However, despite three different auditions, I was left on the 7 p.m. shift.

The problem with the 7 p.m. shift is the men aren't drunk until about 11 p.m., and as every frat boy knows, the last thing you want from your target is sobriety, all of their faculties for logic still intact. *What a drag!* Personally, I liked my men so drunk that they couldn't remember their wives' names, or the value of money, and all they knew for sure was that they were extremely horny, and that I am freaking adorable.

"You look great," Jim told me after I'd walked for my audition. "Go change. We have some paperwork for you to fill out." My stripper dreams had become my stripper reality! *Game on. Let the "agreeing to sexually arouse for money" begin.*

A bouncer, Harry, gave me a tour of the Rhino. He took me out onto the floor. On weekends there was barely standing room in the Rhino, let alone sitting room. My first weeks working, I was constantly being yelled at by bouncers to move because I had no

31

idea where I was allowed to stand. At the Rhino, men can pay for a $20 lap dance out on the floor or head to one of the VIP rooms. All over the room, I watched expensive-looking breasts bounce for paying customers, while men drinking at the next tables looked on for free. I loved the Rhino immediately. This was definitely where the other half partied.

"Where did you work before this?" Harry asked me.

"Nowhere. I just graduated from college. This is my first time stripping."

"Seriously?"

"I thought I'd put my strategic communication degree to good use."

"You're a pretty girl. You should do well," Harry said. I was a novelty. A girl only gets to strip for the first time once in her life, and that night in October of 2010 was my special night. Harry motioned me to VIP Two.

"This is one of our VIP rooms. It's $200 to you for half an hour plus they need to buy two drinks or $400 for an hour, and they need to buy four drinks."

"Okay."

"You can't have sex with anyone," Harry told me. "That includes hand jobs. Don't even jokingly say *yes* when the men ask you for sex or you can be fired or arrested. Don't risk it; we get undercover cops in here all of the time posing as customers. They want to arrest you. The bouncers will make sure you get paid for VIP time no matter what. Don't let the customers pressure you into anything."

"No sex for money. I'll try to remember that." *Aw, how cute am I? I made a prostitution joke!* Harry ignored me and showed me the hundred-dollar room.

"This room is three songs for a $100."

Next, Harry showed me the Champagne Room. Strippers writhed on men inside.

"This is the Champagne room, same prices as the other room. Over here, we have curtained off rooms where it's $400 to you and they need to buy a bottle for $375. Then, each additional hour is $400." Harry pointed at the bar.

"This is the bar. There's also one on the other side."

"What are the rules about drinking?" I asked.

"Don't black out. You could wake up in jail. Don't get so drunk you're stumbling around harassing customers." *Great! I'm going to get a cocktail immediately after this tour. If corporate America had had this sort of drinking policy, I might have placed my bets differently.* Harry and I reached the front of the club.

"Dances on the floor are one for $20. Get the money from the guy after every dance so you know he won't try to stiff you - got it?"

"Yes."

"Okay. Good luck." Harry left me.

That's the onsite job training new strippers get – quick and dirty. Stripping is not a job for the meek. A stripper doesn't have to have a PhD, but she does need to have ovaries of steel. She needs to laugh in the face of approach-anxiety, deal with constant rejection, and beat out a bevy of the world's most beautiful and audacious women. If a girl is not good at talking, I don't care how beautiful she happens to be, she's going home broke. True, once in a blue moon, I would luck out. A man would see me, immediately know that I was the stripper of his dreams, and he'd pull out his wallet while swooping me into Celebrity VIP, but in general, to get more than $100 off of a man, he needed to be half in love, and this required skill.

"Let's get this show on the road." I began canvassing the room deciding which man to approach. The first man I talked to told me he was getting married in the morning.

"This is my first night stripping," I told him. "I have no idea what I'm doing. I'm kind of nervous." I wish I could pull off the whole: "this is my first night ever stripping" spiel every night, because it worked like solid gold. The man took me to VIP for half an hour. I was up $200 right off the bat.

"I don't know what I'm doing," I said during my first lap dance ever. How great is that sales pitch? Unfortunately, it wasn't a line my first night; it was the truth.

"Move slower," the bachelor told me. "The slower you move your hips the better. You're going too fast." Slow is sexy – remember that. I still didn't know what I was doing, and the bachelor tricked me into dry humping him.

"Hey, stop that!" a bouncer interrupted. "You need to move around. Don't stay in one position for too long. You can't do that." *Ah man, this stuff is trickier than I thought… and apparently the advice of men in strip clubs is not to be trusted.*

"You're so great. You make me wish I wasn't getting married tomorrow. We could get together. I'd love to spend more time with you," the bachelor sighed from between my breasts.

"Yeah, it's too bad," I giggled. "I really like you."

I didn't like him. In fact he creeped me out, but he gave me another $100, and I decided I could tolerate him for another three songs. After those songs ended, the DJ announced I was up in two songs for my first stage. Hubby-to-be told me he'd support me through stage and wait 'til I was done to buy more dances.

34

Or not, I thought. *I have magic, first night, stripping powers. I don't need to keep hanging out with a degenerate hubby-to-be.*

I went into the locker room, pulled out my three, crisp, new hundreds and announced to a cute, blonde, part-time nurse that this was my first night stripping, I'd been working only a few hours, and I was up $300. My head was spinning, as I thought about how much work I would have had to do at a normal job to get that kind of money. "A lot" was the answer.

"That's nothing," the little blonde said. "Wait until the nights you make over a thousand dollars." My head was going to explode. The little blonde and I headed back out onto the floor. I told her I was completely sober and about to go on stage for the first time in my life.

"Buy this girl a shot," she commanded a man by the bar. "This is her first night stripping, and she's sober!"

I liked dancing on stage. There were topless girls dancing everywhere out on the floor, and most of the men were busy enough flirting and staring at breasts that hardly any men bothered with the stage sets at the Rhino. Dancing topless in a room packed shoulder-to-shoulder was a rush, and to have most of the men not looking at me felt liberating. If a man without money did make eye contact with me, I could get him to look away by smiling and winking. Men are shy, timid creatures; a girl must approach indirectly in order to not scare them off.

I put my top back on, left the stage, and approached a young group of British men, threw my arms around the guy nearest me, and explained that tonight was my first night dancing. He explained that he was a doctor, and his dad was a doctor, and his friends were doctors, and that he and his friends were in Vegas to celebrate becoming doctors. Two more girls approached his friends.

"Let's all go to Celebrity," the girls suggested.

"Great!" The men agreed immediately - beginner's luck. Two years later, I know miracles almost never happen, but that first night, I couldn't lose. I ended up in a curtained off VIP room with two other topless girls, three European doctors, a bottle of champagne, and a bowl of strawberries with whipped cream. Hell, I'd been to worse parties for free. This party I was making $400 an hour to attend.

My doctor and I were in love for the night - the exact amount of time I liked my post-breakup relationships to last. He was a smart, interesting, kind man, and we had great rapport. Most of the time, I didn't even dance. Instead, I talked with him about politics and life while topless.

"What are *you* doing *here?* My doctor asked.

"A lot of girls secretly want to try stripping, but they don't have the guts," I explained.

"I know, right?" another topless stripper agreed with me. "Isn't that funny?" Actually, it's hilarious.

Finally, I left the curtained VIP at eleven in the morning. I could have stayed another half hour, my doctor wanted to, but I was so sleepy that $200 for the half hour was not enough of an incentive to keep my hips gyrating and my mouth talking.

After paying the club their cut of the dough, over $300 due to 10 percent taken on all credit card transactions, I rolled out into that typically cloudless Las Vegas morning with a huge smile on my face. In my purse rested $1800 - all in crisp, new, hundred dollar bills.

SHOPPING

Well, I'm rich now, I decided after my first night working at Rhino. *What to do with all my millions?*

Shopping was the obvious answer. I bought: Chuck Taylor All Stars featuring Batman fighting crime and thigh-high tan boots from Steve Madden; gold high heels from Guess Marciano; a shirt, skirt, ring, necklace, and purse from Bebe; and I went to one of the nicest salons in town to get my brown hair dyed slightly blonder.

"I'm paying cash," I practiced saying, at different volumes and in different accents, while I skipped merrily about swinging my bags. I listened to the birds whistle *Hell of a Life* from Kanye West's *Dark Twisted Fantasy*:

" *Have you lost your mind? Tell me when you think we crossed the line. No more drugs for me. Pussy and religion is all I need. Grab my hand and baby we'll live a hell of a life".*

I'd found a loophole to getting an entry-level job immediately after college. Thanks to stripping, I knew I'd have ample time to pursue my passions, or at least, I'd have time to discover what they were. But stripping was the little boy with his finger in the dike – not a long-term solution. I wasn't going to be young forever, and my body could only handle so many years of Vegas party life before it raised the white flag of surrender. *What would I do for money when I could no longer stomach all of the tourists gawking and grasping?*

By now, going back to promotional modeling was out of the question. What to do? I thought about the movie *He's Just Not That Into You*, as I always do when I'm trying to make important life decisions. In that movie, Scarlett Johansson was the sexiest woman I'd ever seen. I was jealous of the way she oozed pure sex. What was her job that made men's eyes widen and women want to attack her?

"Eureka, I've got it!" She was a yoga instructor.

Oh my goodness, how great would it be to be a Las Vegas stripper AND a yoga instructor? I would be the enemy of every girlfriend in existence. The last woman in the world you would ever want to have after your man, or woman, was a Las Vegas-dwelling yoga instructor-stripper!

I was going to become Lola from *Damn Yankees* - helping the devil seduce lost souls.

I was going to become the sirens - crushing sailor's ships into the rocks with my irresistible song.

I was going to become old school Britney Spears – my abs the envy of every anorexic cheerleader the world over.

I was going to become a caricature of sexy, and it was going to be a terrific joke.

I got online and searched for yoga training programs. I'd found my calling; the universe very clearly wanted me to go on a three-week vacation to Costa Rica to become a yoga instructor. Indeed, the universe felt strongly that, despite having almost no money, it was imperative I work on my tan, while lying on a beach, sipping water from a coconut. I paid the $200 down payment for the yoga training that day.

GHB AND OTHER FUN DATE RAPE DRUGS

When I first arrived in Vegas I quickly made the acquaintance of Aaron, a devilishly handsome man in his forties who sold party drugs, had two blonde stripper girlfriends, and coached a little league baseball team. What can I say? The man had layers. Because of my short-lived friendship with Aaron, I found myself comforting, not one, but two crying strippers in two different strip club bathrooms advising them that, "It's not you. It's him," and not to put too much thought into the inevitable demise of their relationship.

One night, early in my residency in Vegas, I was over at one of Aaron's houses (he also dabbled in real estate) with a group of people who were playing strip pool and dancing around to electronic music. Aaron offered me some GHB.

"What's that?" I asked (I'm adorable, because I'm from Ohio).

"GHB is a date rape drug," another guy chimed in.

"Sounds great," I said. "Sign me up!"

"No, GHB is only a date rape drug if you take too much," my layered friend Aaron explained. "If you just take a capful, you'll feel relaxed and euphoric."

"Oh, that sounds reasonable."

In Vegas, people take date rape drugs for fun but only in small amounts so they don't get too sleepy, and then, obviously, you should probably balance it out with cocaine. I was a long way from my home.

**

Later that year, I ran into Aaron out at Surrender Nightclub. He told me he was done selling party drugs because, "I have too many crazy girls pissed off at me." Smart guy. Cash out while you're ahead. A lesson we should all learn in Vegas before we end up broke and in prison.

PROMOTIONS

When I first started to work at the Rhino, there were always sign-up sheets on the way in for nightclub promotions in exchange for a free $80 house fee. I loved promotions; they were a great way to meet friends.

For a promotion, girls arrived at the Rhino before 11 p.m. in their best club wear and were given one free drink in the Champagne Room. While strippers in surrounding booths entertained customers, the promo girls sat sipping champagne, deciding, based on friendliness and attractiveness, which girls to be friends with for the night. A hummer limo would come at 11 p.m. and take us to a nightclub on the strip.

The whole point was to create a ruckus. The limo would pull up in front of the casino, and our driver would help us out one by one. We'd walk through the casino en masse, giggling and bouncing, ignoring the stares of tourists in fanny packs. We'd strut past the line, up to the entrance of the club, the red velvet rope would be drawn aside, and we'd be led to our VIP table. Endless bottle popping and happiness would ensue. We'd be given cards for the Rhino that we were meant to pass out, but other than that, our job was to look sexy enough to lure men back to our work where it would be socially acceptable to take their money in exchange for showing them our breasts. At 1:30 a.m., the limo would bring us back to the Rhino. Not a bad gig for $80.

I worked my first promotion on a Tuesday, for an entertainment industry Halloween party at Rain, a club in the Palms. I was dressed as Puff the Magic Dragon: a red and black sequined bikini, dragon paws, feet, and a head constructed from a cut up children's costume from Target.

While we'd waited for our limo in the Champagne Room, I became infatuated by one of the most gorgeous women I'd seen in all my life. She was dressed as a cop, complete with handcuffs and aviator shades. She was incredible: big fake breasts, long thin legs, long brown hair, visible abs, and a face made for TV. I smiled when she caught me staring, and she walked over to join me.

"My name's Kimber. How about you?"

"I'm Laila. This is my first promotion. I've only been in Vegas for a week or so, and I've only worked two nights. I just started dancing."

"How do you like the Rhino?"

"I'm loving it; I made $1800 my first night ever working!"

"Where are you from?" Kimber was all charisma and confidence. I wanted to become her.

"Ohio."

"I'm from Indiana. I've been here for a couple of years. I never go out to the strip unless it's for a promotion. That way you can cut the line and not be hassled. Otherwise, if I have the energy to go out, I might as well go to work for the night."

"Any advice for the new girl?" I asked.

"When you go into the VIP for half an hour or an hour, don't waste your energy dancing the whole time. Hang out talking, and then really start dancing right at the end to get the guy horny. That way, he'll buy more time.

"Tip really well, 25 percent or more, on private dances. That's my best advice. They put girls who tip well on a list to call back to VIP rooms. You'll get VIPs without having to hustle first."

"I'll do that. How much should I tip the DJ? I'm not sure what's a good amount."

"I don't tip the DJ. I pay off-stage every night. Going up on stage ruins my game."

This statement officially made Kimber one of the most badass strippers running around Las Vegas. Working as independent contractors, when dancers check-in at night they have the option of paying the regular house fee of $80, which includes the requirement that they dance on stage for four songs, three of the songs topless, on two different stages, or they can pay $130 to skip their stage set. Practically every stripper takes the first option. However, if you're about to convince a man you've been talking to for 20 minutes to go to VIP, going on stage can ruin your hustle and lose you money. If you're not in good with the DJ, you'll have to leave your mark, and he, and his money, will be gone by the time you're done on stage. This exact scenario played out enough to be frustrating, but more frequently, a girl would pay the extra dough for off-stage, only to end up ruminating in a corner, puffing on a cigarette, wishing she could get her extra $50 back. Only the bravest, most sought-after, girls even attempted this gamble. Kimber paying nightly to keep up a consistent uninterrupted hustle was the mark of a true champion.

At Rain Nightclub, Kimber and I ran around together, drinking, dancing, and having photographers from party websites snap photo after photo of us to prove how great the party had been.

"Come meet the guy I've been dating. He's gorgeous, rich, and French," Kimber said while leading me over to yet another VIP table.

"How did you meet him?" I asked.

"He saw me walking one day and came over."

"Of course he did."

Kimber was an unstoppable goddess. If I could have half the sexual confidence she exuded, then my bank account would be overflowing in no time. We talked to the gorgeous Frenchmen for a while, and I left my new role model to check in at the Rhino table and get another drink.

"How's your night going?" asked a sparkling Tinker Bell.

"Great. This is my first promotion. I'm new to Vegas, and it's nice to have girls to go out with."

"How do you like the Rhino?" Tinker Bell asked.

"I've never had this sort of money before. Do you have any good advice? I can use all of the help I can get."

Tinker Bell became serious as she drew me closer.

"What you've got to do is find out about the man first, before you say anything about yourself, that way you can make up stuff he'll like. Don't talk too much about yourself. No one cares, and why would you want the men to know a lot about you anyway? I massage men's nipples while I talk to them, because it turns them on. Say you can tell he has a really big dick – some men buy that. Another thing that's really important…"

Two Asian men interrupted our conversation. Tinker Bell transformed instantly from con artist to Barbie doll. Her voice raised an octave, and her IQ dropped 30 points. She threw her arms around the neck of the first Asian man and giggle-bounced. *Impressive.*

There was a lot to stripping I had to learn. Luckily, I was studying under the best teachers the seduction world had to offer. The men didn't stand a chance. Their money was as good as mine.

GIVE UP AND GO HOME? DON'T MIND IF YOU DO

As discussed earlier, my college friend convinced me to move to Vegas after we graduated. He'd moved to Vegas right away, while I'd stayed back in Ohio to live out the rest of my lease and followed him three months later. I arrived in Vegas according to plan, and we were on our way. Two weeks later, he reconciled with his girlfriend in Ohio and moved back home. He'd lured me out to Sin City, and then he'd left me all alone. *Great stuff.*

Everything was all right. Don't feel bad. I'd planned on that happening. Moving across the country away from your support system isn't an easy thing to do, and most people are going to go home around month three. This is the time when the newness of the situation has worn off, and the alienation and loneliness have set in and become practically unbearable.

I was only willing to live alone in Las Vegas, knowing no one, because my junior year of high school, when I was 16, I'd been a Rotary Youth Exchange Student for a year in southern Brazil.

My first Brazilian host family would turn up the volume on the television to drown out the sound of me crying in the next room. Who could blame them? I was being melodramatic, and their soaps were on.

My host brother, from my second host family, was constantly trying to have sex with me until the morning I made his girlfriend jealous by giving *my darling big brother* a bikini back massage.

"I'll see you later tonight, BIG brother," I said in Portuguese (wink, wink, cha, cha, cha), before I left for the beach. He never tried to touch me again. Let's hear it for controlling girlfriends. Hip, hip, hooray!

I was constantly under surveillance by the entire Rotary Club of men and women whose job it was to keep me safe and make sure I behaved myself - clearly not my strong suit. Rotary Youth Exchange students lived their lives abroad following the four Ds: No Drinking, No Driving, No Dating, and No Drugs. Breaking these rules was grounds for being removed from the program.

As a result of having a (not so) secret Brazilian boyfriend, with a club of men and women worried I'd get myself pregnant, I was constantly being threatened with being sent back to the USA. If I didn't shape up and fly solo, I could kiss the Brazilian beaches goodbye, and I'd be forced to return to wintertime in the Ohio.

"Damn it, Molly, why is it always so hard for you to behave yourself?"

"Ah shit, Laila, the schizophrenia is kicking in already? I thought we had some time left..."

Alone in Brazil, years before the comfort and connectedness of Facebook, I'd learned I was not always going to be happy, and that's okay because sadness and loneliness have their own merits. During my first months in Brazil, the best I could do was wake up in the morning and keep myself moving until I could finally, thankfully, go back to sleep again. Those first moments upon waking, before my brain reloaded, before I remembered how lonely I felt, were precious and rare. Not only did I not fit in, I wasn't even speaking the same language. Sleep and those seconds upon waking were my only respite. Then, one day, I woke up and everything felt better. Then, one day, I woke up and everything felt great.

Unexpectedly, I became addicted to the challenge of going somewhere new to start over in order to struggle my way back to happiness. In fact, happiness and contentment were sure signs I had grown lethargic and wasn't challenging myself enough. Whenever I became too happy, I'd start itching to leave and try something new – my pursuit of sadness.

"Bring a stuffed animal or something else you can cuddle. You're going to be extremely lonely for the next six months," a woman had told the outgoing exchange students, before we'd left the USA. "It's going to be bad. Mentally prepare for your first months abroad now. Look, I'm telling you, it's not going to be fun. But after those six months, you're going to love your host countries and not want to come home anymore!"

I was miserable a lot of my time in Brazil, but that year was also, hands down, one of the best most-memorable experiences of my life. For a year, I'd lived as a Brazilian girl: I'd taught myself to speak fluent Portuguese, I'd learned to dress as a Brazilian girl, I'd studied at a private Brazilian high school, I'd made Brazilian friends, and I'd fallen in love for the first time with my (not so) secret Brazilian boyfriend.

Then, I went home. I wasn't a Brazilian girl anymore. Actually, I wasn't anything I had thought I was anymore. My year abroad had changed me, and when I looked around my small farming town in Ohio, nothing seemed to be exactly where I'd left it the summer before. My identity as a small town Ohio girl, my identity as a wannabe Brazilian girl, my identity as a Las Vegas stripper, and every other identity I've had along the way, none of it was ever really what *I am*. I realized I am so much bigger than any one identity. I am all of them, and none of them, at the same time. What a blessing, at 17, to have already figured out this fine and fundamental fact of life. I knew I wasn't a stripper (I was, but I wasn't, you see?) anymore than I was a Brazilian girl (America, fuck yeah).

I viewed my half-baked Vegas plan as an exchange year in Las Vegas. I didn't expect to fall in love with Las Vegas. I didn't even expect to be happy in Las Vegas. I never planned to make Las Vegas my home. What I expected was that I would adapt, survive, and eventually, thrive. I'd wait a year or two, until I was happy to be in Las Vegas, and then, I'd get the hell out.

My college friend went back to Ohio and left me all alone in a new strange city, and I was totally cool with that, because I get off on misery and loneliness. I'm not sure exactly why, but ask another writer, and maybe, they can explain this mentality to you.

Now, I needed to find a place to live. I was being kicked out of my friend's house, and I had four days to find somewhere new to stay. And this, meus amigos, is the exact reason Craigslist was invented.

HOW DO YOU FEEL ABOUT ALL-CONSUMING HEROIN ADDICTION?

Many places in Vegas offered month-to-month leases, and thanks to the collapse of the Vegas housing market, the worst hit community in the United States, there were many nice vacant properties in transition. Awful news for the stifled Vegas economy, but great news for me and the rest of the gypsies, tramps, and thieves who were just passing through.

I'd driven out to North Vegas to meet a guy named Ben who had a place advertised on Craigslist for only $425 a month, no lease necessary. Ben and I sat by the pool in his backyard and talked while he smoked a cigarette. A middle-aged Fonzi whose life had gotten sidetracked early on, Ben had slightly graying brown hair, a slim figure, a leather jacket, and grey eyes that always had a scheme brewing behind them. Ben made odd jerky movements, and he looked around in a way that made me feel as though we were being watched. In hindsight, Bobby was probably watching us, but I didn't know who Bobby was back then.

"I meditate over there every morning in the meditation area," Ben told me, motioning with his cigarette to the other side of the pool where Buddha sat achieving enlightenment.

"I try to eat healthy. I used to be an alcoholic, but I've been sober for a long time now. I'm a musician. I have a great music

50

room to show you. Do you play any instruments? You could use the music room."

There was something off about Ben, that much was obvious, but I wasn't picking up on anything malicious, a scam artist of some kind definitely, but he didn't want to hurt me.

Ben showed me around the place, and I was impressed. So big that it was practically a small mansion, there was: a big clean kitchen; a music room with posters of Jimi Hendrix and Miles Davis, and other heroes lining the walls; a giant sunroom with glass picnic tables, cool sculptures, and a lot of space. Ben even had a flashy little sports car parked in the front. I was sold, but what's the catch? Why so cheap? As long as Ben didn't try to sleep with me (and he never did), I'd found myself a sweetheart of a deal. I asked Ben if there was anything else I should know.

"Hmmm... anything else you should know? No, I can't seem to think of anything."

"Well, who all lives here? This is a big place," I asked.

"Well, there's Ed, he lives upstairs, and then there's a couple that lives in that room over there. They're around your age. You'll like them. You guys could hang out."

"And that's everyone?"

"Well, I live upstairs over there. I have a kitchen, bathroom, and everything. I'm barely ever even around this part of the house. Oh, I just remembered something you might have a problem with."

"What?" I asked.

"The couple has a dog. Do you mind dogs?"

"Nope, I have no problem with dogs."

"Well, that's it then!" Ben announced. I gave him $425 and he gave me the door key. I'd found my new home.

THE EVOLUTION OF MY STRIPPER NAME

Whether you're stripping or not, everyone could use a fake name while running around Las Vegas. It's best to be as anonymous as possible in a place where sin is synonymous with culture.

I gave the Rhino the name Kesey. I'd named myself after Ken Kesey, the counter-culture hero and author of *One Flew Over the Cuckoo's Nest*. This book changed the way I perceived the world around me. *One Flew Over the Cuckoo's Nest* is written from the perspective of a big mute Indian - Kesey's psyche on acid. There are great scenes where chairs fly, mist rolls in, and people are eaten in one massive gulp. These dream-like happenings are explained as though they are really taking place. *We're all pretty crazy in our own unique ways* and *don't let them stop you before you've even begun* are some of the main points Kesey was trying to get across. Making my stripper name Kesey was my tribute to the man whose existence had helped me question and come to accept my own lovely breed of madness.

The problem with the name Kesey was, when drunk at 5 a.m. in a Las Vegas strip club, no one could understand what I was saying.

"What did you say your name was?" A man would yell in my ear.

"Kesey!" I'd shout back.

"What?" he'd yell.

"Kesey!" I'd scream.

"Like Easy with a K at the beginning?"

"Exactly!"

"What's your real name?" was always the next question. I hated this question. I needed to give myself a name that at least sounded plausible.

"What's your name?"

"My name is Molly," I answered one night, and I knew I'd found my truth.

My stripper alter ego, Molly, became much more to me than a name. Molly was more than me, because she was free of society's made up rules. Molly was less than me, because the parts of my personality that weren't good for making strip club sales were edited out. Molly was distilled down from the tumultuous psyche of a comedy writer to pure fun, sex, and freedom.

If I ever felt afraid in my life outside of the Rhino, I'd become Molly. Molly was fearless. She could do anything. She could be anyone. Molly didn't give a damn about what anyone thought of her. Molly never felt lonely, or afraid, or heartbroken, ever. Molly never fell in love with men who didn't love her back, because everyone couldn't help but love her. Molly exemplified every sexy, brave, strong woman I'd ever met. A night with Molly was pure ecstasy. Molly will always be a part of me, and for that, I am grateful.

IF YOU WERE HOMELESS, WHERE WOULD YOU SLEEP?

"People think living in a field was bad, but it's not like I hung out in the field all day. I'd always be panhandling for heroin money. I was busy all day. I only *slept* in the field," Bobby said.

Bobby, Tommy, and I stood in a circle passing around a spliff Tommy had rolled with my weed. I would rather be sober than smoke any of Tommy's weed. I believe the strain he sold was called *Gasoline Covered Dirt*.

"That's how I broke my glasses," Bobby said, motioning to his smudged spectacles, held together with electric tape, that were obscuring his blue eyes. "I rolled on them one night when I was sleeping in the field. It sucks. I don't have money to fix them."

Ten years addicted to heroin: five years snorting, five years shooting up, and four years panhandling while living in a field in Vegas, Bobby was amazed by the technology that had passed him by in his time as a heroin addict. He'd admired my computer as something out of a science fiction movie. He'd asked me if 3D movies really looked as though they were coming out at you.

"Shit, I never slept in no field," Tommy said, tapping the ash out of the spliff with chalky black fingers. "There were so many empty houses around Vegas. I slept in a different place every night. Shit, I stayed in some nice places when I was homeless."

I never found out what drug Tommy was addicted to. I figured crack, but it could also have been meth – definitely an upper. Tommy was on some sort of upper today. Usually mellow from the dirt weed he smoked, it was easy to tell when Tommy was up.

Tommy handed me the spliff. I took a hit as I thought about where I would like to live in between panhandling for drug money. I liked the idea of breaking into homes in quaint Vegas cul-de-sacs, but a peaceful field out of the way of traffic also sounded pretty tempting. *Maybe there'd be stars out there in my field...*

It turned out that Ben, the shady landlord, had lied to me. The couple's dog was the least of my worries. I learned that Ben owned houses all over Vegas, and as a sort of side project he rescued homeless addicts from the street and used them to clean his houses. I was living in a sort of bustling halfway home.

"Ben told me I could stay here for free, that he'd give me a home out of the field, if I got off of the heroin," Bobby explained to me once we'd become friends. "I take Methadone now. If you tried to take the amount of Methadone I'm on, it would kill you." Bobby and I laughed together.

"I used to shoot up in the bathroom at IHOP. I wish I was there now," Bobby said.

"Nothing says 'good idea' like shooting up heroin in an IHOP bathroom," I said.

"Shut the fuck up, Bobby, you're going to ruin my day," Tommy said.

"Nah, it was great. Not being on heroin is what sucks. I know where I could get some heroin right now if I had the money. I could call a guy right now," Bobby said wistfully.

"I'm going to go play my guitar," Tommy said. "Thanks for the smoke, Leah." Leah is not my name.

"No problem, Tommy. I'll see you later."

"Put me in your story," Bobby said.

"I will, Bobby. Of course, I will."

Ed the Cat walked up to my legs and stared up at me. I stared down at Ed the Cat as I took a final drag on the spliff.

"She doesn't have any turkey, Ed," Bobby said. "Ed would do anything for turkey. If Ed was a girl, he'd be a stripper for turkey."

Ed the Cat loved turkey, but I didn't have any turkey for Ed, and this is sometimes the awful truth of life.

I'M SO HAPPY 'CAUSE TODAY I FOUND MY FRIENDS

Half of my house knew my name was Laila; the other half called me Leah. I never bothered to correct anyone. I'd answer to both names. Leah was as good a name as any. Eventually, the half of the house that incorrectly thought my name was Leah won, and after those first few weeks living in Las Vegas, I never heard my *real name* said aloud anymore.

Looking back, I've never felt lonelier in my life than those first two months in Las Vegas. My two best friends were recovering drug addicts who used me for my weed and occasionally scammed me out of money, my heart was shredded past recognition, and I didn't meet anyone new other than in the strip club. Strip club interactions started to mess with my head after a while. I learned it's crucial for me to see and have good times with at least two actual friends during the week in between stripping, or it starts to get weird. Like a trip where I don't remember who I am, what I look like, or how to behave in polite society, my weeks would pass without anyone confirming or denying that I existed.

I didn't shower, put on makeup, or shave. I wore old T-shirts and hunched myself over my computer for so long my neck muscles could no longer support the weight of my massive head. I'd eat entire large pizzas in bed while I watched *Internet* TV on my laptop. I couldn't put the leftover pizza out in the kitchen, because heroin addict Bobby would eat my food before I had the chance. I was greedy, and I didn't want to share with Bobby. My messy life sat in rubbish piles around me on the floor.

When absolutely necessary to be awake, I watched an entire semester of lectures for an Introduction to Psychology course from Yale on the website Academicearth.org. While I choked down my tenth slice of pizza, the professor explained to me from my laptop that it's important to have friends, because if we're alone for too long then we might start acting crazy. Friends will check us, point out we're acting crazy, and strongly suggest we stop. Bosom buddies are there to tell us how rotten we are. Naturally, I began to worry I was going insane.

If I go completely out of my mind, and no one is around to tell me, am I still crazy? I wondered.

"Sanity is statistical," Orwell wrote.

If I'm the entire group surveyed, I can never be ruled crazy, I reasoned. *Can't be crazy if I'm the test subject and the control group. It's a statistical impossibility.*

"There are lies, there are damned lies, and then there are statistics."

On weekends, I'd look in a mirror. What a mess I'd be after a week of neglect. I was so ugly. I'd practice my smile. Corners of the mouth up: eh, I can do better. Corners of the eyes up too: looks like real happiness. *You've got this.*

I'd shower, shave, slather on a mask of makeup, put on my lingerie and heels, and suddenly, there'd be a completely different girl looking back at me. She was beautiful - so happy and perfect – so fucking desirable. But I knew she wasn't real. She was in on the joke the world was playing on me. In the daylight, when the neon lights were off, when reality brutally shoved out fantasy, Las Vegas was the ugliest place I'd ever seen.

KIMBER GIVES ME A TOUR OF THE RHINO

"You need to stop acting like a victim," Kimber tells me. "It's not attractive. No one wants a lap dance from Eeyore." Kimber is my favorite character. Based on the real life Kimber I'd met on my first promotion, I'd created her for the screenplay I was attempting, with little luck, to force out of my head and onto paper. If I was going to strip for a living, I would be damned if I didn't get great material out of the whole ordeal.

My fictional Kimber (not to be confused with my actual Kimber) was everything a good stripper should be: a gorgeous, bisexual, sociopath who loves sex, winning at poker, and toying with men. Brown hair, a perfect face, and big fake tits, she was a huge badass, and I was in love with her.

"I'm acting like a victim?" I ask.

Fictional Kimber laughs at me.

"Yeah, girl. You've got victim written all over you. You're like a puppy waiting to be kicked. What happened to you? Did your daddy not love you enough? Did swingers keep you locked in their sex dungeon? Is your pimp forcing you to be a stripper in Las Vegas?"

"No, I just wanted to try stripping, I guess. My ex-boyfriend broke my heart and…" Kimber's not listening to me talk anymore.

"What's your name?" she interrupts.

"Laila," I say.

"Not your real name. I don't want to know that. What's your stripper name?"

"Kesey."

"What?"

"Kesey." I enunciate.

"Like Easy, with a K at the beginning?"

"Yeah."

"That's an awful name. It sounds like some kind of ass toy. Your new name is Molly. You look like a Molly and, if you're lucky, men will give you drugs."

"I smoke weed, but I don't usually do drugs," I tell Kimber.

"Not even free drugs?"

"No." Kimber is pensive.

"'I don't do drugs. I am drugs,' Salvador Dali said that. Did they give you the tour already?" she asks.

"Yeah."

"Useless, right?"

"Pretty much." Kimber laughs.

"Come on, little Molly. Let's get you oriented." Kimber motions for me to follow her.

"Welcome to the Spearmint Rhino. Not only a strip club, the Rhino is an institution. Known world wide for having the most beautiful women money can buy. These women have been in Maxim and Playboy. Some have even been on hit reality TV shows about dating Bret Michaels."

"Wow, THE Bret Michaels from Poison?" I ask in awe. "I wish I could date Bret Michaels."

"I know, right? Everybody wishes they could," Kimber continues. "First thing you need to know. When you're in the strip club, you are the man and the men are the women."

I look around the club, and all of the strippers have become men in boxer shorts, and all of the men are now beautiful women wearing fancy dresses. I watch as the stripper-men try to seduce the lovely men-women.

"What would you do at a normal bar if a man came up and point blank asked you if you wanted to have sex with him?" Kimber asks me. I think back on all of the times I'd gone out in college with a big group of gorgeous girls. Men swarmed all over us, and everything was free on those nights out.

"I'd say no," I answer.

"You'd say, 'Hell no,' and then make fun of him with your friends as he walked away. Same here, you can't just go up to a man and ask him to go to VIP."

Kimber points to a dancer called Diablo – a short-haired punkish girl with a tattoo of a pinup girl on her arm with the words "Johnny's Girl" written underneath. We watch her approach a group of men.

"Do you want to go to VIP?" Diablo asks the men without even a weak attempt at verbal foreplay. The men wave her off. We watch them laugh together as she walks away defeated.

"Horrible game. She'll be lucky to make her house fee back tonight."

Kimber points to a second girl, Alva, an awe-inspiring blonde in a silver bikini. We watch her talk to a bloated man with slicked back hair.

"We are beautiful women," Kimber says.

"I guess."

"Not 'I guess.' Have some confidence, little Molly. We are beautiful women. For our entire lives, men have been lying to us. Manipulating us. Pretending to care while staring at our tits. Now it's your turn. You get to pretend to care while staring at their wallets." We watch as Alva leads her fat bastard to the VIP.

"Convince him you give a damn about him and not his money. That's the easiest way to get his money," Kimber says. She points to a man wearing an expensive, but sensible-looking, watch.

"A couple of things to check for when picking a target: shoes, belt, watch. Expensive and sensible is good. It means he has money."

Kimber and I pass a man wearing expensive sensible attire – a computer programmer? Kimber trails her hand along his chest. He watches her as she walks by swaying her hips. She looks back at him, smiles, and winks. The man tries to figure out how to politely ditch the girl he's been talking to for the last half hour so he can chase this goddess around the Rhino. Kimber points out a man wearing a Rolex covered in glowing diamonds. Three strippers already surround this shiny little man.

"Expensive and flashy is better. It means he has money,

and he spends it on expensive things he doesn't need, because he can."

Kimber and I watch as the man takes the hands of two of the strippers while being led by a third into the VIP.

"Each of those girls are leaving here with at least a $1000 tonight," Kimber says. My eyes glow green. *Those soulless sluts got to him first.*

Kimber and I walk past one of the bars where two black men are standing in baseball caps and baggy clothes.

"Hey ladies, you're looking sexy tonight," one of the men calls to us.

"Hey girl, I like your ass. Come talk to me," his buddy adds. I look at the men, but Kimber ignores them completely and motions for me to do the same.

"Never talk to those men. No one explained to them rappers and ball players had to make money first before they could pick up strippers. Girls aren't looking for broke-ass thugs to take home - only rich ones. Only poor locals and pimps use pick up lines on strippers." We keep walking.

"The next thing to check for with a target: is he drinking?" Kimber points at a man texting on his phone. We watch a bony wisp of a girl approach him, but he ignores her until she gives up and leaves.

"Any man who is sober at arguably the best strip club in the world at 4 a.m. is not worth your time. I guarantee that guy is texting his insecure girlfriend back home that all strippers are whores because none of us like him for his terrible personality," Kimber sighs while shaking her head. "What a loser."

Kimber points at a group of rowdy men – definitely a bachelor party.

64

"To titties!" one of the men toasts.

"To titties!" all of the men cheer in unison before taking straight shots of whiskey.

"Always try and figure out who the bachelor is before you approach a bachelor party, and go for him. Obviously, the drunker the better," Kimber explains. "These men are going to wake up in the morning and have no idea what happened to all of their money."

Transported through movie magic to the bachelor party's hotel room later that morning, Kimber and I watch as one of the rowdy men wakes up. Hung over in bed, he looks in his wallet and is shocked. Another man lays half comatose on the floor, while a third man does a line of cocaine off of the room's glass coffee table. He picks up the remnants of the line with his finger and spreads it across his gums.

"I can't feel my face! This is some good shit!" he whoops to the group. "That taxi driver hooked it up!"

"I had $1000 last night. Now I have $15 and a number from a stripper named Hemingway," the man in bed announces. "I didn't even get laid. My balls are bluer than ever." The comatose man stirs from the fetal position and without opening his eyes mumbles, "Dude, totally worth it. Hemingway was so hot."

The man doing cocaine let's out a triumphant yell.

"Let's go to Rhino again tonight! Who wants a morning line? Vegas, baby! Let's go gamble!"

Movie magic takes us back to the Rhino, and Kimber points to a group of Italian men having a conversation with animated hand gestures.

"Foreign men will ask you for sex. They don't mean to be rude; they don't understand that American strip clubs aren't brothels. This helps getting them back into the VIP. By the time they realize that not only are they not allowed to fuck you in VIP, they can't even touch your pussy, you already have their money."

We're by a table of Asian men. Every man here is getting a lap dance from a blonde stripper.

"Asian men love blondes, so you should dye your hair blonde. You'll make more money," Kimber tells me as she brushes back her brown tresses with a perfectly manicured paw.

"Your tits are already great. Are they natural?" Kimber asks.

"Yes."

"Some guys might be into that." We watch a stripper bend over in front of a man with a blank bored expression on her face. By the time she's turned back around, her face has changed to radiate lust. The man's eyes lights up like a child's on Christmas morning as he focuses, laser-like, on her nipples.

"How much everyone loves breasts has always fascinated me," Kimber says. "American society is cruel. For the first year of our lives breasts provide comfort, nourishment, and life itself. Breasts are the epitome of goodness; they embody all that is right with the world. Then, suddenly, we're told breasts are evil, dirty, and forbidden. Meanwhile, half of our celebrities are idiotic whores, little girls are given half-dressed dolls to play with, and everyone's obsessed with *Internet* porn. Thanks to this double-think, religious, shame-based culture, strippers, like us, are able to make terrific money just for showing our tits to the sexually-repressed masses. Breasts are a fantastic niche market."

Kimber points to the stage where two girls are dancing and doing pole tricks.

"No matter how weird this job becomes, always remember this is *not* a dream. A girl was fired once for dropping her panties and taking a naked shit on stage in the middle of her set. When the managers asked her what the hell she'd been thinking, she said she'd thought she was in a lucid dream, there were no real consequences to her actions, and she'd be awake in no time. I shit you not."

Kimber and I enter the locker room. The lockers are covered in stickers: "I Make Boys Cry," "Good Girls Don't, But I Do," "If You Don't Have Any Money Take Your Broke Ass Home." Strippers dress, primp, sleep on chairs, and eat Ramen noodles. Kimber gestures to a box.

"This is the Rhino's Lost and Found. If you find any money lying around, or if you see a man drop anything, just bring it back here so he can claim it later. 'Thou shalt not steal.' That's one of the Ten Commandments." I'm confused, and Kimber laughs.

"That was a joke. Vegas is a enormous gypsy camp, but instead of traveling around to find new suckers, the rubes come to us. Anything you find is yours. Watch your stuff. Don't keep valuables in your locker. Keep them on you. I've seen men lose wedding rings in here, and girls get their purses stolen during lap dances."

"What you want to do is fold your money in half long ways, then fold it around your shoe in the middle, and secure it with a rubber band." Kimber points to the thick wad of hundred dollar bills tied around her shoe. Tina, a voluptuous Brazilian blonde, enters the locker room.

"I had a man take me into Celebrity VIP for four hours! I'm up almost $2,000!" Tina says to Kimber.

"Great job, girl!" Kimber says. Tina smiles and turns to her locker.

"Never brag about your money. It's how you make silent enemies," Kimber says. She points at two girls who are now glaring at Tina's back. "Buy yourself a good lock."

67

"Speaking of money," Kimber says, "Don't believe what the other strippers tell you they make. Everyone inflates their income to inflate their worth. Usually you'll be able to make a thousand in a night or two, but on unlucky weekends, a thousand might take three nights to make. If you work with the bouncers to have them call you back to rooms for a cut of your money, you can sometimes do better than that." We head back out onto the floor.

"Finally, watch out for cops. Two girls were arrested last night for prostitution." Kimber points to a tall man standing in front of a framed picture of a big breasted blonde. Mindy, a curvaceous Indian girl in bright purple lingerie and large white heels, approaches him.

"Hey," the man says to her, "I'm organizing a bachelor party for tomorrow night and want to find some girls who would eat each other out or whatever - lesbian sex. How much would that cost? We can pay really well." Kimber and Mindy roll their eyes in unison.

"No," Mindy says, "I don't have sex for money. Sorry and good luck."

"Never say *yes* when a man asks you if you'll have sex with him on the floor. Personally, I don't have sex for money, unless it's a really great offer, I value my health too much, but some girls do. If prostitution is something you want to do then wait until a man has spent money on you in VIP. If he tries to finger you without asking first, then you'll know he's not a cop, and you can make plans to meet him outside of the club."

A leggy copper-colored goddess in tan lingerie approaches Kimber from behind. Without saying a word, she wraps her arms around Kimber's waist and bites her neck. Kimber closes her eyes and tilts her head away from the bite with a sigh. The copper goddess spins Kimber around to face her, and the two begin dancing. The men stare. I hold my breath - mesmerized. The vixen stops her lips just millimeters away from Kimber's ready pout, she looks at me from the corner of her eye, our eyes connect, and she

68

holds my gaze effortlessly. Her eyes dance, lighting up around me, and she smiles. I can barely breathe. She straightens and turns to face me.

"Who's this?" she asks Kimber.

"This is Molly. It's her first night ever stripping, and I've decided to help. Isn't she cute? My maternal instincts took over." The girl comes over and begins to touch my breasts.

"You're really hot, Molly."

"Thanks."

"Are these real?"

"Yeah."

"Huh, some guys might be into that. I'm Miss Berry."

Kimber puts an arm around my waist and says, "Molly, how would you like to make $1000 in the next 4 hours?"

"Are you joking? That would be amazing!"

"Good because you're going to make $2000. We were gambling with some French men earlier tonight and they're coming in to party with us." Miss Berry laughs.

"Welcome to fabulous Las Vegas, Molly!"

LIES MEN HAVE TOLD ME

1) "I'm a poet. I keep a box of poetry under my bed. Come up to my room. I'd love to read you some aloud."
2) "I can tell you're not like all of the other girls."
3) "My dad is the Bill Gates of wine. I want you to like me for my personality and not my money."
4) "I don't want to have sex with you. I just want to share the cocaine I have in my hotel room with you."
5) "I just want to cuddle."

LIES I'VE TOLD MEN

1) "That's so interesting you're a poet. I'm sure your poems are great!"
2) "I can tell you're not like all of the other guys."
3) "I think you have a great personality. I couldn't care less about your money."
4) "I only have time to stop off in your hotel room for a minute. My friends will worry about me if I'm gone too long."
5) "I haven't had sex in months. I'm so horny right now."

SAPPHIRE'S COMFY BEDS

Occasionally, when I first started, I'd strip at Sapphire – the only club in Las Vegas said to rival the Rhino. I don't have much I care to write about Sapphire. The girls were great-looking, and everyone was nice to me. Seeing the night manager of Sapphire caused me to squeal with joy and give him a big hug, as he'd ask me, "How have you been sweetheart? I haven't seen you in a while."

This management strategy was a lot different than Jim's, the night manager at the Rhino. Jim struck terror into the hearts of most of the girls and lowered the self-esteem of the rest. I didn't blame Jim. Keeping the world's craziest hot women under control was no easy task. Every night, at the Rhino, there was a new line of stripper-hopefuls waiting for Jim to judge. Not to get high off of that sort of power would be nearly impossible. You never doubted who was in charge when Jim was around. He'd purposefully given half the Rhino girls complexes about their appearance. He was infamous. When I was in Miami for Ultra Music Festival and said I worked at the Rhino, the man I was chatting with asked me if I knew Jim and claimed to be a great friend of his. There are men all over the world claiming to be great friends with Jim.

While the Rhino barely had standing room, Sapphire was built in an old warehouse where there was nothing but space. Since no one could sit at the Rhino, I was on the same level as the men.

I'd make laps around the club until I made eye contact with a man, and then, I'd go for the gold. In Sapphire, all of the men sat at tables, and seemed wary of any girl trying to interrupt their conversations. I felt like a waitress selling lap dances instead of lattes.

I had come to view stripping as a sort of bizarre girls vs. boys battle that played out nightly. Sometimes, the girls would win, and other times, the boys would come out ahead. At Sapphire, no matter how much cash I took home, I always left feeling as though I'd lost. The one thing I liked more about Sapphire than the Rhino was the bed in the locker room.

**

One night before work, I was sitting smoking a bowl of weed with Bobby in the kitchen.

"Would you like a Xanax?" Bobby offered me. "It'll make you feel really relaxed and happy while you strip, but don't drink." Well, that sounded good to me. Abusing Xanax's prescription-strength calming powers could only be good for me. Having grown up in America's generation RX, I believed no problem, even if it wasn't my problem, should go un-medicated.

"And though she's not really ill, there's a little yellow pill... What a drag it is getting old."

Bobby had a Xanax prescription, but with the amount of Methadone he was on, the additional strain of Xanax could kill him. However, this risk wasn't enough to stop him from taking the Xanax. I couldn't judge him this weakness. After sleeping in an open field for four years, once you've been addicted to heroin for so long, the options come down to living clean and starting a life over from scratch or dying. And hell, dying can't be all bad. I took the Xanax from Bobby right before he passed out with my bowl sitting in front of him.

**

That night at Sapphire, I popped the Xanax and began my rounds. It wasn't working out. There's nothing relaxing about hustling men while wearing lingerie and glitter heels, and now I'd foolishly made it so I wasn't able to drink. I went back into the locker room to fix my makeup. On my way back out, I stopped to look in the mirror.

"Are you all right?" A girl asked me.

"Why?" I asked.

"Well, you looked as though you were about to pass out, and then you almost fell over, and then you snapped out of it and started walking again." Preach, girl! She was speaking the truth.

"You're right. I'm going to go lie down." I passed out immediately on a bench between the lockers in the middle of stripper traffic. Apparently, with Xanax, it's important to get the prescribed amount right...

The week before, I'd lived it up in New York City: I'd stayed with an investment banker friend from college in his swanky West Side loft, had VIP tables at the nicest clubs, drank champagne midday at the museum of Modern Art, watched the Broadway shows Wicked and Avenue Q, and I'd eaten at some of the world's best restaurants. Now, I was passed out in the back of a Las Vegas strip club.

"Classy as fuck," as we used to say in college.

A kind-hearted stripper woke me up.

"Don't sleep there," my savior told me. "There's a bed in the other room."

The confusing girl-shaped blob led me from the bench into another room with a bed where four strippers were already passed out together under blankets. At last, I'd found *my people*. I spent the rest of my shift having a lingerie cuddle session with the

73

wayward lovelies who were too intoxicated and irresponsible to be Las Vegas strippers that night.

Wait? Wasn't stripping in Vegas supposed to be a sort of joke? My personal, "Fuck you," to the status quo and everything I had been told I *should* be doing with my life? The joke was on me. I'd found where I belonged, and that place was passed out on a bed in the back of a Las Vegas strip club. When I finally woke up, I left down $30, but I will forever be grateful for the bed in the back of Sapphire. A little lost girl only has so much party in her before she needs a long nap.

I LOOK EXACTLY LIKE A SPORTS ILLUSTRATED SWIMSUIT MODEL

I knew I needed to move out of that shyster Ben's house, because of my housemate Bobby's poster.

I was sitting with Bobby in the large sunroom, smoking weed. As usual, we were talking about all of the places he'd shot up heroin, when Bobby said, "Leah, you've got to check out this poster. It looks just like you."

"All right, Bobby, let me see it."

"No, it's down in my room. You need to come check out the poster in my room."

"Nah, I'm not going all the way down to your room, Bobby."

"Why not? Come on, you've got to see this poster!"

"I'm too sleepy from all of the sleeping I've been doing. I can't walk that far, Bobby. Bring it over here if you want me to see."

"Leah, come on, I want to show you the poster," Bobby begged. I wasn't afraid of Bobby. Bobby was a nice boy from Ohio who had made a series of terrible decisions. I just really, quite sincerely, didn't give a damn about his poster. I relented.

Bobby and I walked over to his room, and he pointed to the only thing hanging up in his nearly barren garage bedroom – a picture of a bikini clad Sports Illustrated swimsuit model. The girl in this full-sized poster had one hand suggestively pulling down on her bikini bottoms and the other hand thrown helplessly behind her head.

"See, she looks just like you!" Bobby said.

"Kind of, Bobby. She looks a little bit like me, I guess."

"No," Bobby insisted. "She looks *exactly* like you! I showed Tommy earlier and Tommy said she looks like you too."

"Whatever, Bobby, let's go smoke more."

"You don't think she looks like you? That model looks *exactly* like you."

Bobby was really doing a nice job turning his life around when I moved out. He had new glasses his family had mailed him from Ohio, and you could see he was actually a pretty handsome guy underneath all of the junk that had been destroying him. He wasn't always talking to me about heroin anymore, and it had been over a month since he'd passed out at the kitchen table. He was still mooching my weed more than ever, but occasionally he would find the money to buy a little bit of his own *Gasoline Covered Dirt* weed from Tommy and would offer, as a pretense, to smoke that with me. I was proud of Bobby, and I genuinely liked Bobby.

But, the facts were, a recovering heroin addict who did not have a computer or the *Internet*, and had limited chances to leave the house because he had no form of transportation, had a poster of an almost naked girl he believed looked exactly like me. A lot of masturbation was going on to that poster.

I had to tell landlord Ben that I was moving out as of the end of the month. Since I'd moved in, almost two months before, Ben had fallen off of the sobriety wagon and had returned to being a volatile alcoholic. I tried to find a time when Ben was sober, because I didn't know how he would react to the news of my departure while drunk. I'd always made it a point to wait out his screaming alcoholic rages in my room.

"FUCK YOU BOBBY!" I'd hear Ben scream as he rampaged through my door. "YOU'RE FUCKING USELESS! I'M GOING TO FUCKING BEAT THE SHIT OUT OF YOU, BOBBY!" I'd cower under my covers and wait for them to shut up and make up. Then, I'd go in the kitchen and make myself a sandwich.

I expressed my concern for my safety to Tommy over a joint in his room one day. Tommy sat on his cot holding his guitar while I sat on a straight-backed wooden chair. A weak light at ground level dimly illuminated the barren space.

"Don't worry, Leah. No Leah, no cry," mellow as yellow, not-on-uppers-today, Tommy assured me. "You're fine. Ben would never yell at you. He just yells at Bobby, but I know Ben, and he's never yelled at no girl."

Thus assured, I told Ben I was moving out.

"You're the real deal, Leah - a true artist," Ben said. "You're going to be great. Good luck on your journey."

I had earned the belief of Ben, a true-to-life musician, a lifelong artist, and an alcoholic who regularly went to Mexico to "fuck the girls there."

"Leah," Ben explained, "You get paid a $100 for three topless dances in Vegas. In Mexico, I can do whatever I want to a girl for less than $50. And I'm talking *anything*. You girls won't do anything at all for $50! I would never pay more than $50 for a girl."

I found a furnished room near the strip and McCarran airport on Craigslist for only $450 a month, everything included. I would be able to drive to work in 15 minutes, and a taxi ride to the airport would only be $10. The family of a German girl, Amy, who studied at UNLV, owned the apartment. Amy was sweet, cool, enjoyed cleaning, and loved house music. We added each other on Facebook, confirmed everyone was who they said they were, and I told her I'd move in the first of January. Amy and I went to the electronic music festival, Electric Daisy Carnival, together; she always offered to drop me off at the airport; I took care of her puppy, Yoda, when she was out of town; and once, she brought me a fruit smoothie in bed. I lived with her for the rest of my time in Las Vegas, and my home life became blissfully uneventful.

MILLIONAIRES ARE IDIOTS TOO

I watched a 27-year-old, self-made, *Internet* millionaire as he put down a $200 chip on the blackjack table in the Wynn's high roller room.

I'd only met him that night, through a mutual friend in town for an *Internet* marketing conference, but I knew we were going to be in love forever. Tall, dark, and handsome, a Ferrari, and a shiny Rolex watch - he was definitely my soul mate. I watched my dream man win two consecutive hands.

"Awesome!" I cheered him on to victory. I am Lady Luck.

"Yeah," he said, "But whenever I put down $1000, I lose. Watch."

In 30 seconds, I watched him lose $1000.

No! My brain screamed in silent horror. I stared at the massive pile of chips about to be squandered and wondered if there was a way for me to liberate that money. *Just one $1000 chip… he probably wouldn't even notice it was gone.* I decided not to steal his money, because I'm a decent human being, or because a bouncer would have tackled me to the ground before I'd completed my daring escape.

"Let's take a break," my soul mate suggested. "I've been gambling all afternoon." We left the table and went to have a complimentary drink at the high roller's bar.

"I lost $12,000 at the Rhino last night," he said to me.

"What? How did you spend that much money?" I asked him while kicking myself for having stayed in bed smoking weed, eating pizza, and watching terrible romantic comedies on Netflix instead of going to work the night before.

I hadn't told my future husband I was a Rhino stripper, but if I was planning on marrying him, I saw no point in telling the truth. I didn't want to create unrealistic expectations for the rest of our lives together. I'd told him I was a Rhino waitress instead.

"Well, when I got there, three girls asked me if I wanted to go to the VIP with them, and I did, and I stayed in there for three hours. I didn't realize I had to pay for it!"

Maybe we're not soul mates after all, I realized sadly. *He's clearly some sort of idiot savant with amazing business skills, but he otherwise suffers from a complete disconnect from reality.*

"What? You thought the Rhino gave you bottles of champagne, strawberries with whipped cream, and three strippers out of the kindness of their heart? You're lucky you're good-looking, because you're a complete idiot."

"That's not the worst part! Those trashy whores stole $6,000 from me!"

"You're a trashy whore," I countered smartly. *I guess there are other fish in the sea. If only it could have been me stealing this kid's throwaway cash.* I sighed wistfully at the thought.

"They didn't steal your money, you owed them money for three hours in VIP," I explained slowly.

"No! That only cost $6,000! I had another $6,000 cash and they must have taken it out of my pocket, or maybe the money fell out, and they didn't tell me, and they kept it. Fucking thieving whores!"

"Did you check the Lost and Found in the back of the Rhino?" I asked.

"The Lost and Found?"

"Oh yeah, whenever a guy loses anything at the Rhino, and one of the girls picks it up, they always put the money or item in the Lost and Found. That's probably where your money is now."

"Really?"

"Fuck no. Next time, don't walk blackout drunk into a den of thieves with $12,000 cash in your pocket."

"Whatever. Stupid whores."

Yeah, something like that…

In one weekend, I watched this guy spend $12,000 at the Rhino, and he lost another $35,000 gambling on blackjack in the high roller room, the equivalent of the average American's yearly wages spent exclusively on gambling and strippers.

"If you've seen it once, you'll never be the same again."

SAVED A WRETCH LIKE ME

In my first two months in Las Vegas, I'd saved up enough money to go on a 21-day, 200-hour, vinyassa flow yoga certification program in Costa Rica.

That January, I slept on a bunk bed in a dorm-style room with five other aspiring instructors. All together, we were 26 people in my training, ranging in age from 21-to-65. I felt pleased with myself, because the only other two girls my age were a gorgeous actress from London who was able to use money from a national pizza commercial for the training, and a girl whose dad was a martial arts health guru living on an organic farm outside of Toronto. Thanks to stripping in Las Vegas, I was able to become one of the world's youngest yoga instructors.

Every morning, we woke up at 6 a.m. and got ready for the day in contemplative silence. Serenaded by howler monkeys, and escorted by peacocks, we'd walk to the dining area by the pool for morning tea. From there, we sat in a circle together and meditated for 30 minutes. Next, we had a two-hour long yoga practice, then three hours of yoga instruction, which was followed by a two-hour lunch. The program had employed a gourmet vegetarian chef from New York City, and every meal was my new favorite meal. During the two-hour lunch break, we studied Sanskrit, practiced our teaching, relaxed by the pool, and played in the ocean. After this, we had three hours of yogic philosophy. Next, we'd have dinner followed by enough homework to last until 10 p.m. when it was lights out. We repeated this schedule 21 times, and then I was officially a certified yoga instructor.

The women in the program grew close to one another and spent hours talking about our respective lives. I told them I was working as a waitress at the Spearmint Rhino in Las Vegas. They all felt I needed to be saved. Maybe I did, but I didn't have enough money or know-how yet to earn my salvation.

"One of the observances of the Yoga Sutras of Pantanjali is Bramacharya, or abstinence. Today, we interpret Bramacharya as having respect for our sexuality and not using it to manipulate others," my instructor said while she stared directly at me. I looked over my shoulder to see who she was speaking to. The critique didn't faze me. If I hadn't been able to make money by manipulating men with my sexuality, then I couldn't have been vacationing in Costa Rica being criticized by righteous yoginis for my skewed moral compass.

I'd developed a cough the first week of yoga training. My lungs were clearing from the constant smoke inhalation of months camping out in my Las Vegas bed – the physical manifestation of my mind's weakness. Since we were sharing such close quarters, everyone was worried about catching a cold from me. I had to explain I was quitting smoking and wasn't really sick; I was healing.

I'd grown so used to being completely alone my first months in Las Vegas that the lack of privacy in Costa Rica was overwhelming. Suddenly, there were 26 other people around me constantly analyzing my every move and expression.

"Are you sad?" the girls asked me. "You look upset."

Talking to other people was hard but good for me. By the end of my training in Costa Rica, my psyche had done a complete turnaround, and I felt as though I'd been given the road map to a happier, healthier, more spiritually fulfilling life.

I no longer felt alone. I was music! I was the OM! I felt better than I'd ever felt in my life, and I was willing to do whatever I needed to do to continue feeling this utterly blissful. I decided I would no longer eat meat (which surprised even me) because I wanted to hang on to this light wonderful feeling, and if that meant changing my eating habits then that was a tiny price to pay for the new Laila I'd found in the jungle. With my head clear for the first time in months, I also resolved not to smoke marijuana anymore.

"You look like a completely different girl than the one who came here!" a kindly grandmother yogini complimented me on the second to last morning of the training.

"Thank you!" I said appreciatively. She was right. I'd rebuilt some shoulder and neck muscles, and I was standing as straight as an arrow. I'd gotten the rot out of my lungs, and thanks to relaxing poolside, instead of skulking around Las Vegas strip clubs, some healthy color had returned to my face.

That night, we had a bonfire on the beach. Everyone brought fire offerings to share with the group: poems, inspirational quotes, stones that take the pain away, and coconuts hacked from trees. During morning meditation, I'd failed to clear my mind, and instead, silently composed a list for my offering, which I read to the group beside the fire.

Things I learned @ Frog Lotus Yoga International Teacher Training January 2011 @ Goddess Garden in Costa Rica

- Ahimsa means non-harming. Every animal and plant on Earth is sacred and beautiful... other than mosquitoes, which are the scourge of the planet. Mosquitoes must be destroyed swiftly and without remorse.
- When men are out of the equation, I revert to the age of 11 and farts become super hilarious again.
- Peacocks, raccoons, dogs, and other wildlife have the right-of-way.

- The old "I accidentally locked myself in my room" excuse for missing morning yoga asana practice can, unfortunately, only be used once.
- Bowel movements should be discussed for a minimum of five minutes every day to compare and contrast with others and reassure yourself you are normal.
- "Pa… pa… pa…" mumbling something under your breath does not trick anyone into thinking that you've done your Sanskrit homework.
- It's hilarious to say: "Now, step gracefully forward into Bird of Paradise."
- Practicing Brahmacharya, or abstinence, is a lot easier when I'm isolated in the Costa Rican jungle with almost exclusively women.
- A warm shower is a privilege, not a right.
- Don't announce what you're going to do. Do it!
- We are all strong, fierce, warrior Gods and Goddesses!

Everyone laughed, crowded around to congratulate me, and took turns trying to sit by me on a log by the fire. They asked me to send them the list.

"I thought you were shy this whole time. You seemed so timid," said the gourmet vegetarian chef. "And then you stand up and do that! That was great!"

Having so many wonderful friends telling me I'd made them laugh felt incredibly good.

I'm going to be okay after all, I thought with a smile. *If I can make this many good people laugh, then I'm going to be okay.*

A group of four of the girls and I took our coconuts away from the fire and out to the Ujjayi-breath of the ocean waves.

"We're going to put the past, all of the negative feelings, all of the bad energy into this coconut," said a gourmet chef from Norway.

85

"The stress will leave our bodies and flow into this coconut," said a mother of two from Wisconsin.

"And then we'll throw the damn thing into the ocean!" cheered a lawyer from Vancouver.

"Perfect," smiled a stripper from Las Vegas. I closed my eyes. I breathed along with the waves. I pushed past my recent traumatic past and came into my present. I launched the coconut into the ocean with all of my newfound strength. I looked up at the stars, and I laughed.

I received so much more out of my time with those wonderful men and women in Costa Rica than a yoga certification. As we studied yogic philosophy, learned about Patanjali's 8-limbed path to Samadhi, and talked about the OM and our oneness with everything, I discovered that yoga was what I'd been searching for my entire life. Yoga was everything I wanted in a life philosophy; it was everything I already passionately believed, but had never had the right words to express, even to myself. I could workout barefoot as a spiritual exercise, and sharing my passion with others would make them healthier and happier. Yoga seemed too lovely to be true. I'd started my yoga training as a lark, and to my surprise, I'd found peace and a group to which I could finally belong.

ALLERGY SEASON AND THREESOMES

Upon my return from Costa Rica, I found a job as a yoga instructor with Las Vegas Athletic Clubs, one of the largest, best, gym chains in Las Vegas. The yoga instructor who hired me said my application came at the perfect time as just that week another instructor gave notice to go work on an organic farm.

"I've been feeling pretty sick these last couple of days," I told a student as I left from teaching one of my very first yoga classes.

"It's allergies," he told me.

"Really? I didn't realize there was anything in the desert to be allergic to."

"Oh yeah, there's all sorts of stuff floating around the air."

That night, for Saint Patty's day, I took some medicine to soothe my headache and went to Tryst Nightclub for a Rhino promotion. All of the girls met in the Champagne Room as usual, and I picked out some friends for the night. Soon enough, we were escorted to and then from our limo, flounced past the line (ignoring the stares), walked up to the bouncer, through the velvet rope, and over to our VIP table. *Whoa-man, sometimes, I really dig Las Vegas life!*

The next weekend, I had my flight already booked to Miami for Ultra Music Festival, and I needed to save up as much money as possible at work that weekend.

"I'm going to drink enough so I'm in a happy horny mood at work tonight! Then, I'm going to take everybody's money!" I told the man in charge of the promotion. He smiled broadly, congratulating me on my full-proof plan.

That's the last memory I have of the night.

**

I woke up in the bed of a chic Bellagio hotel room. I moved back the covers. I was naked.

"Oh, shit." I covered my face with my hands and peaked through my fingers to discover who I was in bed with. There was a man.

"Oh, shit!"

I looked past the man to the woman.

"Oh, SHIT!"

What the hell did I do last night? My naked bedmates began to stir.

"Good morning," the man said warmly with a French accent. He was in his forties, blue intelligent eyes, full head of slightly graying blond hair, and blond stubble.

"Good morning!" the woman - lovely, thin, blonde, also about forty - added.

"Last night was magic, don't you think?" the man asked.

"Yes, last night was magical!" the woman enthused.

"OH, SHIT!" I laughed and put my head back in their new shameful home of my hands.

"I don't know how much I remember, but I'm sure last night was pretty magical."

"You don't remember last night?" the woman said in amazed disappointment. They were both so excited about our night together, I felt rude letting them know I had no memory of meeting them, let alone of having had sex with them.

At least they're attractive, I thought. I was grasping at straws.

"I think my allergy medication mixed badly with the alcohol..."

"I'd never been with a woman before last night. It was amazing," the woman said, stretching out naked on the bed in remembered ecstasy.

"Last night was your first night with a woman? A threesome happened with two women and a man, for the first time, last night." I clarified the situation.

"Yes, she kept saying how exciting it was to touch a woman. How soft you were to kiss," the man enthused.

"Last night was my first time with a woman too," I said.

"I don't believe you," the woman said.

"I wouldn't believe me either. I don't appear to be the most responsible person..."

"I'm going to shower!" the woman said as she hopped out of bed, entered the bathroom, and closed the door. The man stood and went to the foot of the bed.

"I want to have you again right now," he said as he opened a condom and spread my legs. I couldn't remember meeting this man, and didn't know his name, but considering I'd already had a *magical* threesome with him, it seemed rude to say *no*. How do you go from a carefree tryst that started at Tryst to saying, "Ew! No! Who are you?" I had to think fast and find a polite way out of morning sex. I pointed at the bathroom door.

"Isn't your wife in there?" I asked.

"Yes, she's fine with this," he said.

"Are you sure?"

The man's face briefly flashed pain. This was a secret that hurt to share.

"Yes, she was with another man some months ago. That is why she is okay with this." I looked past him, staring hopefully at the bathroom door towards my salvation.

"I don't know," I said. The man sighed heavily.

"I'll go ask her." He stood up naked and entered the bathroom to ask his wife if it was okay for him to have morning sex with the 22-year-old lying naked on his hotel room bed.

I took in my surroundings. A dozen roses were in a vase on a counter. A mostly empty bottle of champagne with three glasses sat beside the bed. *Well, that helps explain my lack of memory.* The man reentered the room.

"She says we can have sex!" he said happily. The wife reentered the bedroom in a bathrobe, jumped on the bed, and kissed me on the lips. It was nice. Women are so soft.

"She doesn't believe you're okay with this," the man addressed his wife.

"Better you than me in the morning!" the wife laughed before reentering the bathroom, leaving me alone with her husband. *Oh great.* The man came back over to the bed, put on a condom, and climbed on top of me. I faked enthusiasm - the only time I've had sex out of a sense of propriety. When we'd both finished, I climbed out of bed, and began the morning after scavenger hunt for my belongings. The wife reentered the bedroom, naked and clean, from her purifying shower.

"You will come to breakfast with us?" she asked.

"Okay, yeah, at this point, I might as well get breakfast," I said.

"Fantastic! And then we can go dress shopping!" the man said.

"Oh, dress shopping! You're such a lucky girl!" the woman said.

"The luckiest," I pouted.

"And lingerie. We can buy lingerie. After breakfast," the man added.

"Yes, we'll go shopping for everything!" the woman said.

We headed down together to Café Bellagio. I sat across from my new married lovers in my dress from the night before, disheveled, with no makeup on.

"So what do you do? Was your name Molly?" the man asked.

"Yes, I'm Molly. That's my stage name. I'm a dancer here in Vegas. I was out at a promotion last night when I met you both. I meant to go into work, because I need money for a trip to Miami I'm taking next weekend, but... I guess... I met you two instead."

"A Stripper? Completely nude?" the woman asked.

"No, only topless. In Vegas, you can only serve alcohol if the club is only topless. If the club is fully nude, it's not allowed to serve alcohol. I wouldn't be comfortable having my vagina out and exposed to the elements."

"In Paris, where we're from, we don't see being topless as a big deal," the woman said.

"In the United States, we're raised to be ashamed of our bodies. It's better for the economy if we all hate ourselves," I said. "What are your names?"

"Chantal," the wife said warmly. The man was clearly hesitant to tell me his real name, as though I was going to go to Paris on a righteous crusade to besmirch his reputation. All is fair, I suppose, I hadn't told them my real name either.

"Daniel," he said.

"A pleasure to meet you both."

Chantal took out her phone to show me a photo.

"This is our daughter. She's 3-years-old."

"She's beautiful."

"Her name is Fernanda. She's a princess. She gets whatever she wants," Daniel said proudly.

"I'm sure she does."

"We didn't mean to have children," Daniel added. "It's changed everything. We never wanted to have children."

"This is a photo of us in Cabo. We were there a month ago." Chantal showed me the photo. "Cabo was very beautiful. I bought a very beautiful bathing suit while we were there."

"You'll have to show it to me."

"You modeled it for us last night!" Chantal said.

"Of course I did. What do both of you do for work?"

"I'm a surgeon," Daniel said with the closed composure of someone telling a partial truth. I was making my living in half-truths and lust; I could smell my own.

"A surgeon. Impressive."

"I'm a Pilates instructor," Chantal said.

"Oh really? That's great! I'm a yoga instructor. I teach during the week."

"I love yoga!" Chantal said.

"Are you a vegetarian because of the yoga?" Daniel asked.

"I eat fish. It's okay to eat fish, because they don't have any feelings. That's what Nirvana said at least."

"Us too. We only eat fish. As a surgeon, I know it's much healthier to not eat meat," Daniel said.

"I try to be very healthy. I do yoga every day, I meditate, and I eat well."

"This was lucky," Chantal said. "We are a nice couple. This is the first time we've done something like this, and you're a nice girl – a yoga instructor. I'm glad you were who we met."

"You're very beautiful," Chantal told me admiringly.

"*You* are beautiful," I said. Chantal was lovely inside and out. She was the type of woman I always love, a born mother. Chantal looked unsure of my words.

"She doesn't believe she is beautiful," Daniel said with barely concealed animosity. Infidelity, threesomes, and belittling one another in public – these are all signs of relationship apocalypse. I'd drunkenly stumbled my way into the middle of the death throes of a Parisian couple's marriage.

"What? Of course she's beautiful."

"If I were to ask the men in this room if they want to have sex with her, most of them would say *yes*," Daniel said.

"*All* of them would say *yes*. I said *yes* last night. She's gorgeous." I turned toward this kind insecure beauty, and stared into her eyes.

"You are gorgeous," I said. Chantal looked embarrassed.

"She won't believe," Daniel said accusingly. "She won't believe she is beautiful."

"Don't be silly. Ugly women do not have your life," I said. Chantal laughed.

"Seriously, ugly women aren't married to handsome surgeons. They don't pick up Vegas strippers for threesomes. They don't go on vacations to exotic locations, or have lovely princesses for daughters. Only beautiful women get to have this life."

Daniel smiled, "I tell her this all of the time."

"That's enough. I don't want to talk about this. I don't want to believe it's true. I prefer to think I am normal."

"You don't gain anything by behaving as less than you are. You are incredible."

We finished our breakfast and walked over to The Forum Shops at Caesars Palace to go shopping. Chantal wore high heels and a mini skirt.

"Daniel likes me to dress this way," she explained. We walked underneath of the domed ceiling painted blue with white fluffy clouds.

"I prefer the real sky to this," Chantal said.

"But this one is better, because this sky is more expensive," I said.

We walked into Guess Marciano, where I tried on dress after dress until finding a $200 white dress so formfitting it appeared as though I'd been the model they'd fitted the garment on. Daniel bought the dress for me. We next headed to Victoria's Secret, and I picked out a $100 set of lingerie. Daniel bought the white lacy garment for me, and a matching set for Chantal. We walked through The Forum's impressive display of luxury, and Daniel put his arm around me.

"Would you spend tonight with us?" he asked.

"Honestly," I answered, "I would love to. I've really enjoyed you both, but I'm going to a three-day music festival in

Miami in a couple of days, and I really need to go to work to make money. I don't have the money for my trip yet."

"How much would you typically make at work?" Daniel asked.

"On a good night, $1000," I said.

"I'll give you $1500 to not go to work and come out with us instead."

"Yup, I'm in."

"Great!" Daniel said. "Chantal, Molly is joining us tonight!"

"Oh really? That's wonderful!"

**

At 7 p.m., I stood in the lobby of the Bellagio wearing my gold glitter heels, the purse I'd bought myself from Bebe after my first night dancing at the Rhino, my new white dress, and new lingerie - a total cost of $550. Easily the most expensive outfit I'd ever worn, I ignored the stares of everyone around me. I concentrated on my phone and waited for Daniel to retrieve me.

"There you are. You are perfection," Daniel said, putting his arm around me. We headed up to his hotel room. We entered the room, where Chantal, standing in her bra and underwear, clapped her hands, and jumped up and down.

"How are you? You look so beautiful!" She approached, and we kissed hello – truly so lovely. "You don't have any jewelry on?"

"I didn't have anything beautiful enough to go with this dress," I said.

"YOU are the beautiful thing that goes with the dress," Chantal said.

"I'm going to take a shower," Daniel said, heading into the bathroom. Chantal put on music.

"Let's dance!" she said.

"Yes!" Chantal and I danced around to the music, laughing, and playing.

"Look at this dress!" Chantal said, grabbing a work of art from her bag. She placed it on the bed, and we lay on either side of the garment, lovingly caressing the fabric.

"The dress is Chanel," she said.

"It's incredible," I said. I watched sadness come into Chantal's eyes.

"Are you happy?" I asked her.

"Sometimes," she said. "Sometimes, I'm happy. I know he affords me a lifestyle I couldn't have without him, but I don't know..."

I nodded. My poor, fragile beauty - I wished I could protect her from the teetering house of cards she'd built as a life.

"I lied when I said you were the first woman I was with," she confided. "I was with my friend Christina months ago. Christina is my best friend! She's wonderful! You'd really like her! Daniel doesn't know. He doesn't like Christina." A storm brewed behind her green eyes.

Daniel exited the bathroom.

"I'm going to wear this dress tonight!" Chantal said, selecting a white dress.

"No, wear something else," Daniel said. "I don't want you both to wear white."

"But, I want to wear this dress," she said.

"No."

Chantal went into the bathroom to put on her makeup and put in her hair. Daniel took my hand and led me to the window. He sat me down in front of him and held me from behind. We watched the Bellagio fountains shoot water and light into the air.

"This is so beautiful. You are so beautiful," he said. "I think this moment will be hard to forget."

"Yes."

"I want to keep you forever," Daniel whispered in my ear. I stared past my reflection down to the fountain below.

Chantal exited the bathroom, and Daniel jumped back from me.

"Don't do that!" Chantal scolded. "I don't want Molly to feel uncomfortable."

Chantal put on a blue and orange dress.

"Did you notice the fourth glass?" Daniel said mischievously to Chantal.

"Because we found you last night, Daniel said I can find a man for tonight. I'm thinking a large black man." We all laughed in shared conspiracy.

**

We approached the hostess of Alizé, a five star French restaurant at the Palms.

"The reservation is for two. There are three of you now?" the hostess asked.

"Yes. Now, there are three of us."

For dinner, Daniel ordered us all a seven-course meal paired with a different wine for each course selection. The meal cost well over $1,000 for the three of us, and to this day, dinner at Alizé remains the most fantastical meal of my life.

"I'm a plastic surgeon. I have 15 people who work for me," Daniel divulged more of his life.

"My real name is Laila." I reciprocated. Our original apprehension had evaporated.

"Laila!" Chantal said. "What a beautiful name!"

"For a beautiful girl," Daniel said as Chantal nodded.

"Look at her nose!" Daniel said. "Her nose is perfect."

"Yes, her nose is perfect," Chantal agreed.

"And your lips are so lovely and full," Daniel continued.

"Thank you."

"And your breasts! They're wonderful. If you came to me and said that you wanted a breast job, I would tell you *no* and send you away. Not every plastic surgeon would do so, but I wouldn't operate on them."

"I've had some surgeries done," Chantal said. "Daniel did my cheeks for me, and my chin. I like my breasts. They're little, but I like real breasts."

"Your breasts are wonderful," I said.

"My friend Christina, she's wonderful! She has wonderful breasts! She's so lovely! She's my best friend!" Chantal glowed.

"No, she's ugly," Daniel spit venom. "Christina is awful. She's stupid and ugly. She is terrible."

I reasoned Christina must have played a part in Chantal's recent infidelity. Regardless, it was obvious Chantal's affection for Christina far surpassed that for her husband.

"No, she's lovely," Chantal said quietly, scolded, looking down.

"It's good for Chantal to see a woman who likes herself," Daniel said.

"I love myself," I said.

"You're going to be a great woman," Chantal said.

"Thank you," I said, looking down at my food. "I'm trying to be."

"I mean, you are. The way you think, it's so different."

"If I could have anything for our daughter," Daniel said, "It would be that she is independent. I think a woman having her independence is the most important thing." Daniel noticed Chantal's grimace and showed some mercy.

"The younger generation is different than ours," he addressed Chantal. "We had different values in our day, but now women must be as strong as the men and make their own way."

Next, we went to Rain Nightclub at the Palms, and Daniel brought us champagne. We all danced together as a threesome, and led each other hand-in-hand around the nightclub. A tall, drunk, bully of a man called me over to him.

"Sorry, I'm with them," I said.

"Both of them?"

"Yes, both of them."

"I want sex all of the time, and she only wants it once a week. It's hard," Daniel complained to me in front of Chantal. Daniel couldn't see his wife's lack of desire for him as anything other than her fault. He was infallible.

Chantal left and began her search for a large black man. Daniel held my hand as he jealously eyed her scouting the floor. The same monster douche that had tried to grab me started dancing with Chantal. Out of all of the horny Vegas tourists, Chantal had chosen my least favorite man in the room. I loathed him on principle. Daniel bristled. In a desperate attempt to regain the esteem Daniel had stolen, Chantal began to kiss the swollen frat boy.

"Get off of her!" Daniel yelled, running over, and pulling Chantal away.

"Hey man! What the fuck?" the brute yelled back.

"That's my wife!"

"Your wife is a whore!"

"Fuck you! You have no idea what you're talking about!" All 120 pounds of me yelled up into his ugly face. We got away from him, and I tried to reestablish friendly relations between Chantal and Daniel. Apparently, a large black man would not be joining our night after all.

"We're going to Boston for my work in several months," Daniel said. "You must join us. You and Chantal can go shopping together while I have my meetings. It'll be like I have two wives!"

At 3 a.m., we took a limo back to the Bellagio. Laughing, we burst into the hotel room.

We helped each other out of our clothes. "I've never gone down on a woman before," Chantal said. "I want to."

"Yes."

I watched her blonde head as she kissed down my stomach to my pelvis. This time, I remembered everything.

In the morning, I woke up to Daniel touching me. As his wife slept beside him, he fingered me until I came.

"Do you think the separation will be hard?" Daniel whispered in my ear. "If I was ever to be alone, I would want a girl like you - a beautiful, young, independent girl - and then start a family."

I looked past him to Chantal sleeping.

"I have so many chances to be with other women. Women want me all of the time, but I always say *no*. I wonder how hard it would be to leave her. You must stay in touch with us. I'll give you my email, and you need to write us."

No, I couldn't. Poor Chantal. This would be the last time I would ever see them.

Chantal began to stir, and we all enjoyed our last morning together.

"Thank you for everything."

I got dressed, and we hugged.

"Make sure you write us!" Daniel said.

Chantal handed me a rose, and I kissed them both goodbye: I headed out of the hotel room, down the hallway to the elevator, and through the casino to the valet. I waited for my car, tipped five dollars, and then drove to the gym to teach a morning yoga class.

ULTRA MUSIC FEST: YOGA AND RAGING PROPER

A blog post written for a friend's music website, March 2011

Please allow me to introduce myself: I'm a woman of wealth and taste... ha, not quite. But here's what I am: a college graduate of June 2010 who couldn't stomach the idea of using my communication degree to sell knives door-to-door.

Upon graduation, I packed up my car and drove cross-country to seek my fortune in Fabulous Las Vegas.

How's life in Las Vegas? Weird. Yesterday, I was lying on a sofa, watching a movie, contemplating how Angelina Jolie is so perfect, when a Vegas strip headliner's wife burst in wearing a Mexican wrestler mask and tried to coerce me into giving her a lap dance. This is normal for Vegas.

I'm a yoga instructor and an electronic dance music fiend, and I just got back to Vegas from *The Best Party Ever* in Miami: Ultra Music Fest. I do not use *The Best Party Ever* label lightly. When I was 16, I raged hard for days on Laguna Beach in Brazil, widely regarded as the best Carnival in southern Brazil: dancing on the beach, no Americans in sight, samba dancing my heart out with exchange students from around the world, all while drinking underage. Ultra was equally mind-blowing.

I want to share my Ultra experience, one of the best of my life, with all of you from the lens that I viewed it through: Patanjali's eight-limbed path of yoga.

The first yogic limb: Yamas

Yamas are guidelines to living life with universal morality. Patanjali talks about five of these, and I'm going to write about one - Ahimsa or non-harming. Over 100,000 people were in attendance at Ultra, and there were no fights. Bump into someone?

"Sorry," you say.

"No problem," they say.

The two of you begin dancing together.

An amazing amount of respect for everyone permeated the Ultra experience. Everyone was dressed in his or her most outlandish rave wear, and everyone was quick to compliment the ingenuity of new friends. There was no vulgar grinding. If you met a handsome girl, or guy, then the two of you danced; you really danced. If you did touch, it was beautiful, rhythmic, a celebration of the present moment.

I danced for three songs with a gorgeous boy.

"I'm already in love," he said to me after the first song.

After song three, he smiled and said, "I'll see you on the other side!" We hugged, and then he danced away.

The 2nd limb: Niyamas

Niyamas are personal observances to lead a spiritually fulfilling life. Patanjali discusses five of these, and I'll explain one, Ishvara Pranidhana, surrender to the absolute. Holding an asana, yoga pose, for 12 long slow inhalations and exhalations teaches you to relax and to surrender. When you surrender to the pose, you're able to sink deeper, and you experience the stretch, and life, on a new level.

At Ultra, you must surrender to the music. If you fight the music, stay in your contracted shell of neurotic mind chatter, you're not experiencing the music correctly. Let the music wash over you. Enter you. Surround you. Surrender to the blissful unity of dancing full force with a huge group of like-minded people.

The 3rd, 4th, 5th, and 6th limbs: Asana, Pranayama, Pratalyahara, and Dharana

These four limbs are: yoga poses, focusing on your breath, cultivating control of the senses, and one-pointed focus. While dancing at Ultra, all four of these limbs came into play. Yoga has made me a better dancer with crazy backbends and utilizing the full movement my body is capable of. Breath control helps keep the rhythm flowing. Controlling my senses, and one-pointed focus, allow me to focus on what's important: my body moving in unison with the vibrations all around me.

Devote all of your thought to what's truly important to you. Watch as the obstacles fall away.

The 7th limb - Dhyana

Dhyana is meditation. Every morning, I sit for 30 minutes meditating. Meditation works by focusing on my breath and welcoming the silence. Whenever thoughts, memories, worries, whatever, intrude in the peace, I label them. I say *thought*. I say *memory*. Labeling the mind chatter helps me to become aware of the way my mind works.

Yoga is a moving meditation, and meditation is about being present; experiencing what is happening *right now*. At Ultra, I experienced the importance of remaining present. My body was busy dancing, but my mind was busy worrying. As I danced, I worried. My thoughts went to the men I'd loved, the mistakes I've made, and how disappointed I am with myself for being merely a selfish animal…

Then, I remembered the silence and the control.

"No, this is the past, and the future, but none of that matters, none of that really exists. The present matters. What is happening RIGHT NOW?"

I snapped out of my funk, looked around, and RIGHT NOW I was dancing full throttle beside some of my best friends in the world. One of my friends was giving a tripping girl a light show with his dayglow gloves while he danced. MSTRKRFT was playing some of the dirtiest beats a dirty girl like me could ever ask for.

The present moment was (is) incredible!

The 8th limb: Samadhi

Samadhi is the goal of yoga, and for me, the goal of music. Experiencing a connection with the energy of everything, understanding we are not alone, we are all connected, and hopefully, if only for a moment, we can feel the vibrations of our own bodies lose their rigid boundaries, and we become one with all of the vibrations, of everyone and everything, around us.

I've lost myself in music and experienced Samadhi, that yogi coveted experience of vibrations, energy, and unity, so many times. The pursuit of Samadhi is what keeps me returning to shows, and keeps me dancing with everyone who will dance with me.

At the end of the second day of the three-day Ultra experience, Deadmau5 had everyone begin clapping. We all clapped at different times, out of synch. Deadmau5 began to play a beat; we all clapped in perfect unity. The music brought us together, and together we all danced. My own body no longer mattered. All of us together, experiencing the exact same moment, was more real than anything I've ever experienced. Finally, we were all one with the music, and the energy, and our lives on this planet that is our home.

Party on, my friends. I'll see you next year in Miami.

Q: WHAT ARE *YOU* DOING *HERE*?

Correct answers include, but are not limited to, the following:

A: I'm a Girl Scout. Once I make over $100,000 stripping, I earn my seduction badge. I'm going to sew it under my camping, origami, knot tying, and breaking and entering badges.

A: I'm here spreading the word of Jesus Christ. Have you accepted Jesus into your heart as your lord and savior?

A: I'm helping support breast cancer awareness. That's why I'm wearing this green plastic bracelet saying, "I Love Boobies."

A: Lap dances are green. I'm trying to keep my carbon footprint minimal by selling a service instead of a commodity.

A: I got laid off from my job selling knives door-to-door, and AFLAC wouldn't hire me unless I agreed to pledge allegiance to that damn duck.

A: Stripping is a form of protest against the patriarchal establishment. I burned all of my bras, and now, I have no choice but to go topless.

A: Stripping is a mitzvah.

A: I like the uniform.

A: I'm a nymphomaniac. I've tried to get help, but the urge to have anonymous sex with tourists is too strong to always resist. Against my better judgment, I'm back here again tonight... let's go to VIP?

A: Flexible scheduling, competitive earnings, and sometimes, I orgasm while on the clock.

ON MY GRIND

At the beginning of the night, I caught a man's eye and walked over.

"How are you?" he said in a familiar accent.

"Where are you from?" I asked.

"Brazil," he said.

"I love Brazil," I said in Portuguese.

"You speak Portuguese?" he responded.

"I lived in Brazil for a year," I continued in Portuguese. "I was a high school exchange student." I always did great with Brazilian men. Often, they could barely speak English, which narrowed their choices for the night's stripper down to me... or me. I was in. He took me to the three-for-a-hundred room.

"I really like you," he said. "Do you like me?"

"Yes, of course I like you," I said.

"I know this is usually fake, but it's not fake for me. Is it fake for you?"

"No, it's real for me too."

"Will you come visit me in Brazil? You can stay with me and we can go out to all of the clubs. I live in a very nice place."

"I'd love to come visit you."

The songs ended, and the Brazilian and I parted ways. For the rest of night he stared at me from afar. Twice he stood possessively by me while I danced for other men – a betrayal of our real feelings for each other. Before he left, he grabbed me for another three-for-a-hundred dance to reaffirm our love before reluctantly leaving me behind.

"Is it real for you? It's real for me. Is it real for you?"

"Yes, of course. It's all real." I approached a man I'd seen staring at me from his chair. I leaned over him and smiled.

"Let me dance for you," I breathed into his ear.

"Absolutely," he sighed. I took off my bra, placed it next to me on the floor, and I began to dance.

A second man stumbled by, stopped, threw up on my bra, and continued his inebriated journey across the club.

"Oh no!" I shouted. Molly, jarred out of her lap dance trance, stared down at my defiled undergarment.

"What?" The man's focus deviated from my breasts down to the floor.

"That guy just threw up on my bra. Oh well, don't worry about it." As any performer knows, the show must go on.

When the song ended, I grabbed the bra, covered my chest with my arms, and tore through the crowded room to the Rhino's stripper store.

There's a store in the Rhino where strippers can buy new lingerie, jewelry, purses, fuzzy boots, shoes, and makeup. Men aren't the only people drunkenly taken advantage of in the Rhino. There were many nights, after having easily made hundreds of dollars out on the floor, a drunken 5 a.m. lingerie splurge became a great idea.

"A man threw up on my bra. I need to buy a new one," I informed the woman standing behind the counter full of cheap bling. I placed my bra on a lip-shaped chair.

"Don't put your vomit bra on the chair. Pick it up. That's disgusting. I'll get you a plastic bag," the woman scolded me.

"Sorry," I said, ashamed.

I stood topless in the middle of the store, holding a bra covered in puke, waiting for the woman to retrieve me a bag. When she returned, I placed the bra in the bag, and topless, began perusing new two-piece lingerie. I settled on a turquoise swimsuit with bows and skulls.

"While we're here, you should buy me that sparkly hand-cuff necklace I've been wanting," Molly insisted.

"Fine, Molly, but only because you've been through the ordeal of your bra being thrown up on. I concur you deserve something shiny for the mental distress you've suffered."

I bought the necklace. A quick trip to the locker room to wash my bra, tuck it away in my locker, change into my new garb, and I emerged a different, slightly shinier, Molly. Once more, I began to circle the floor.

A group of British men stood laughing and talking at the bar. I maneuvered into the side of their circle, and targeting a handsome tall Brit in glasses, I gave a welcoming smile.

"How are you?" I asked.

"Great." He smiled. "How are you doing?"

"Pretty, pretty good," I said. The fatherly Brit pulled out his phone and showed me a picture.

"These are my daughters," he told me proudly. "They're about your age."

"They're lovely," I told him.

"Yes, they're great girls," he said. "Very smart girls. Here, this is for you," he said as he handed me £50 – a $73 value at the time.

"Wow, thank you. Did you want to get a dance?" I asked.

"No, that's for you, but thank you."

"If you're not getting a dance, then I want one," his friend made a move towards me.

"No, the money is for her," he scolded his opportunistic buddy. "I hope you have a good night."

I spotted a man sitting with a group of friends wearing a shirt featuring an adorable kitty shooting lasers from its eyes. Perfect.

"I dig your shirt," I said as I slid onto his lap, "Because I like kitties and lasers."

"Why thank you," the man said. "What's your name?"

"Molly. And you?"

"Dan."

"A pleasure." Frenchy walked by and touched Dan's shirt.

"Meow," Frenchy winked and scratched Dan's arm.

"Did you already talk to her?" I asked.

"She sat with me earlier," Dan said. "She really likes cats."

"She was on Rock of Love," I said. "You know, that TV show about dating Bret Michaels on VH1. A bunch of girls who work here were on those shows. They must have had casting calls straight out of the Rhino. The girls probably got two free house fees for being on a Vh1 program."

"So what do you do?" Dan asked.

"I'm a yoga instructor," I said. "I teach during the week and dance on weekends."

"I'm going to graduate school for psychology. My mom is a yoga instructor. My college is very spiritual. We do meditation exercises and spiritual studies."

"I try to meditate every day for half an hour. It's amazing how much meditation changes the way my mind works. Getting upset is almost impossible when I meditate regularly." I said. "When someone does something bad to me, then I think, 'How does this make my body feel?' and I examine the reaction. When I'm not meditating and someone does something against me, I think, 'How could they have done this to *me*?' Meditation gives me a quiet place I can return to."

"Yes. Exactly. Wow," Dan said.

"I control my thoughts. My thoughts do not control me," I said with a smile.

Dan and I talked for the next half hour about psychology and philosophy. I danced two songs for him, and he gave me $100.

"Did you want more dances then?" I asked.

"No," he said. "I know I wasted a lot of your time where you could have been making money."

"Not at all. Talking to you was a pleasure. And you bought me drinks that have fortified me for the rest of my night. Thank you." I kissed Dan on the cheek and headed back out onto the floor.

I began to approach a brown-haired man in an expensive suit. He looked me in the eye and waved me away from him with one hand. I switched course. I approached a blonde man, smiled, and slid onto his lap.

"Did I tell you, you could sit down?" He asked, frowning at me.

"No, you didn't." I thought maybe I could still salvage the situation. "I'm Molly. What's your name?"

"I'm not interested. I didn't say you could sit down." I stood up and continued my search.

I approached a distinguished-looking, older, European man. Another girl approached his friend, and with some coercion on her part, we all headed to the VIP for half an hour.

I sat topless, straddling the European.

"Can I lick your armpit?" he asked.

"My armpit?"

"Yes." I considered the request.

"I don't see why not." The European man licked my armpit.

"That felt incredible! No one has ever licked my armpit before," I said.

"Really? Never? I love it. Can I do it again?" he asked.

"Yes, please! Do it as much as you want!" He licked my armpit again.

"You're ruining me for other men. How am I ever going to get someone else to lick my armpit?" I asked.

"You are so beautiful. I usually don't like these tease bars. What's the point? I get so excited and then nothing. But, with you, I understand why one would like this." I stopped dancing and took a drink.

"Thank you," I said.

"How much to get you to my hotel room?" he asked.

"Sorry, that's not for sale."

"Ah, so you're a good girl," he said.

"I'm the best girl."

"Come on, how much? $1,000? $2,000? You're incredible."

"I'm flattered but no."

"Come on. I'm not a cop. I'm European."

"Touché." The European man pulled out his wallet and removed a hundred dollar bill.

"Here's another hundred for you. This way you understand money means nothing to me." I took the money gratefully as the European man replaced his wallet.

"Thank you. You should lick my armpit again." He did.

"I have houses all over the world," he said. "You can stay in any of them you want. Do you want to go to Brazil? Thailand? Anywhere."

"Brazil would be nice. I could be the girl from Ipanema."

"And a car," he sweetened the deal. "I'll get you a car. What kind of car do you want?"

"An expensive one."

"Of course, only the best for you," he said. "I think I'm in love."

After the half hour, I left the European, and the DJ called me onto stage. I started dancing, and off to the side, a group of women cheered me on. They all held up ones, calling me over for entertainment.

"Motorboat me!" a woman yelled. I obliged, drawing her head between my breasts.

"Me too! Motorboat me too!" another woman yelled. Women are great when they're enjoying themselves instead of glaring at me. I obliged woman after woman as they handed over ones.

"Do your parents know what you're doing?" one of the drunken women asked, looking very concerned for my soul.

"Not yet. I'm going to tell them when the book is out. That way they can skip being upset and, hopefully, go straight to being proud of me."

"What?"

"Nothing."

"How old are you?" the woman asked.

"Way too young to be doing this. Stripping is destroying my innocence," I said as I did topless cat-cow yoga breathing in front of her. *Exhale as you tuck your chin in towards your chest and arch your back up towards the sky as though you're a little pussycat...* The woman was appalled.

"Do your parents know what you're doing?" she asked. Drunken women are so cute when they repeat themselves.

"Yes, my mom and dad are both strippers. Stripping is the family business," I said.

"Oh, I guess it's okay then," she said. Her face broke out in a smile.

"You want to be motorboated too, don't you? Don't be shy," I cooed.

The woman nodded. I motorboated her, and she gave me a big appreciative hug. I stood up and, blowing her a kiss, danced over to the pole to do a combination spin-back bend.

When I left the stage, a man from India grabbed me.

"Let's go to the three-for-a-hundred room," he said with a thick accent.

I took his hand and led him to the VIP room. He paid me, sat down, and I started to take off my bra.

"Don't do that. Leave your bra on. I want to talk to you," he said. *What the hell?* I looked enviously around at all of the other women writhing topless on top of their customers.

"Are you sure?" Confused, I reclosed my bra. He barely spoke English. *What was he doing?*

"No, I don't really like that. I like to listen. I want to know everything about you. Tell me about you."

Suddenly, I understood. I placed my fingertips together ala Montgomery Burns and sat down beside him.

"Excellent."

I'm positive this strategy is written in a handbook for men trying to have free sex with strippers, because frequently, I'd have men offer to give me money "just to talk." The idea, I gather, is the stripper will be so flattered the man sees her as anything other than a sexual object, she'll let her guard down and forget she's a set of hired tits and become temporarily human again. This lapse in game can cause the stripper to become vulnerable. Then, the man will be able to take her home with him as a reward for being such a *great guy* that he was able to see past her stripper persona to the *real girl* underneath. Fucking diabolical.

This strategy only works out on the floor, not in the VIP, and only on newbie dancers. The rest of us will simply pretend to believe you really like us, take your money, talk for half an hour, and then leave you to go hustle up more dances.

Guys, this is what we do for money. With amateur status, you simply can't compete.

The Indian man was royally screwing up the pickup routine. He had made the quite comical mistake of paying me to talk in a time-controlled environment. I was being forced to make small talk with a man who barely spoke English, because this idiot thought, after we left the VIP, I'd get a copy of his hotel room key and ask what reward he would like for listening to me talk about my childhood memories. The three songs ended, and we headed back out onto the main floor.

"You'll go to dinner with me tomorrow night," the man commanded. I laughed in his face and walked away.

I slid onto the lap of a man in his thirties wearing a blue shirt.

"Hi, I'm Molly," I said.

"You're really pretty Molly, but I've already spent all of my money. Sorry. You can hang out here if you want, but I can't pay you."

"Okay, have a good night." I moved on.

I spotted twins, broad shouldered and broad jawed, bright green eyes set in olive skin, late twenties, sitting side-by-side along a wall. They were very handsome, and therefore, I assumed, broke and arrogant. But I decided I should talk to them anyway, because there were two of them, and because I'm worth it.

"So where are you two sexy men from?" I smiled as I slid on to the lap of Dreamy Twin One.

"New Orleans," Dreamy Twin One answered.

"I lived in New Orleans for a while," I said.

"Everybody says that," Dreamy Twin Two said.

"Everybody, except me, lies."

I made eye contact with Dreamy Twin Two, and my heart began to beat faster. I bit my lower lip and smiled.

"So what are you doing later?" Dreamy Twin Two asked.

"Dry humping men for money. It's a terrific quad work out. You?"

"I'd love to go down on you," Dreamy Twin One offered.

"We'd both love to go down on you," Dreamy Twin Two added. I raised my eyebrows.

"We have so much in common!"

"Then, come to our hotel room with us darling. We'll take turns eating that pussy like it's never been eaten before."

"I don't want to have sex with either of you. I want you both to go down on me, and then, after I've gotten off multiple times, I want to go home, and watch Breaking Bad."

"That's what we want too!" Dreamy Twin One said.

"We'll pay you $50," Dreamy Twin Two added.

"Fifty dollars?" I said, incredulous, "You've got to be joking me."

"Darling, if a woman told me she'd blow me for $50, I'd say, 'Hell yes, and you can keep the change,'" Dreamy Twin Two offered. I laughed.

"Being a man must be so hard."

"Darling, you have no idea."

"All right, boys, this has been stimulating, but I've got to get back to work. There are old rich men out there waiting to meet me," I said as I stood up. "Good luck finding a girl."

"Thanks, darling. You're beautiful."

I approached a man in his mid-thirties with a baldhead, a big honest smile, and stylish Prada shoes.

"Hey there, I'm Molly!" I said with the enthusiasm of a circus clown.

"I'm Anthony!" his enthusiasm equaled mine.

"So what's your story, Anthony?" I asked.

"Well, I'm from Australia. Sydney. I own a chain of physiotherapy centers."

"A whole chain? Kind of overachieving, don't you think, Anthony?"

"I have a lot of energy," Anthony explained. "I need to keep busy, or I get into trouble."

"We have so much in common."

"I'm here with one of my employees," Anthony gestured to the Aussie standing next to him engrossed in whatever the stripper with raven hair and pink lingerie was whispering in his ear. "I told him I'd buy him a dance. What do the VIP rooms cost?"

"Did I pick the wrong friend?" I asked Anthony.

"No, of course I have to get a dance from you. Well, wait. Give a spin." I spun.

"Yes, I'm getting a dance from you."

"Dances are $400 for an hour, $200 for half an hour, and we have rooms that are only $100 for three songs."

"Let's start off in the three-for-a-hundred." I grabbed his hand, and the other girl and I led our Aussies to the VIP.

"So what do you do other than dancing?" Anthony asked as we walked through the crowd.

"I'm a writer," I said as we reached the VIP.

"A writer? My favorite writer is Oscar Wilde. I'm a bit obsessed," Anthony said.

"*The Picture of Dorian Grey* is one of my favorite books. I wish I had a painting to take on the wrinkles and ugliness of my misdeeds. I could stay young and up to no good forever." Anthony's eyes shined brighter. I ignored him as I approached the bouncer.

"That'll be $100 for each lady." The bouncer shined his light on Anthony's hands. Anthony obliged and pulled out two hundreds.

"This is one of my favorite Oscar Wilde quotes," I said as I took off my bra and turned around.

"The only way to get rid of temptation is to yield to it." I sat down on his lap and raised my leg up next to my face as I leaned back into him. "Resist it, and your soul grows sick with longing for the things it has forbidden to itself."

"Who are you?" Anthony exhaled.

"I'm Molly."

When the three songs ended, Anthony happily forked over another hundred for the stripper with his friend and me, and we continued with a mix of dancing and talking for the rest of our time together.

When the dances ended, Anthony headed back to his hotel room, and I spotted a boy even younger than me. He needed to go home. He had no idea who he was, where he was, or what he was doing.

As I watched him, how lost he was, I thought of every girl who had ever been taken advantage of when they'd reached the dangerous state this boy was in. I thought of every man who had ever seen a woman lost to the world and decided they were going to have sex with her body. I thought of every frat house, bar, and bedroom where girls made themselves into easy targets for creeps… like me.

"Well, what are you waiting for? He wants it. Why else would he be stumbling around dressed that way?" Molly goaded me forward.

"Anyway, he won't remember any of this in the morning. You're in the clear." I made my approach.

"Hey sexy, how are you tonight?" I said. I put my arms around his neck.

"I like you!" he said.

"You're exactly who I was hoping to find tonight."

"I like you," the boy repeated as he tried to grab my breasts. I caught his hands.

"Let's go to the VIP and get a dance."

"Okay!" the boy said.

"Where's your wallet? Do you have money?" I asked.

"Yeah!" He took out his wallet. I looked inside.

"You only have $50. We'll need more than that," I said helpfully.

I half carried the girl to the ATM line. I propped him up against my arm to keep the bouncers from taking him away from me. The remaining part of his brain sensing danger, he broke free of my talons, darted away, and tried to exit the Rhino through the emergency exit. Luckily, I was able to catch him.

"You can't go out there," I scolded. "Don't you like tits?"

"Yes," the chastised boy said.

"Don't you want to see mine?" I asked.

"Yes!" I led him back to the ATM line. He attempted to escape again, but this time I was ready and grabbed him.

"I told you, you couldn't do that!" I said. "Now I'm mad."

The poor boy was sad he'd upset me - the little bitch.

"I'm sorry."

"It's fine. Where's your wallet?" He pulled out his wallet.

"Give me the $50 you owe me, and I won't tell a bouncer what you did." He stared blankly down, oblivious.

"You owe me $50," I repeated. "Don't make me get a bouncer."

He handed me the $50 from his wallet.

"Thanks," I said, before I left him to fall down. "That was fun. I'll call you."

I spotted Aaron, the guy who drank GHB for fun, dated two blonde strippers, and coached a little league baseball team. He was looking as handsome as ever.

"Hey, good to see you," he said. "We're about to head down the road to Cheetah's if you wanted to join."

"Definitely. It's 7:30 am, and I've had a good night. I'm up about $800 and could use a morning cap."

I met Aaron and a couple others down the road at Cheetah's, a strip club that's a far cry from the Rhino. At 8 a.m., there were only three girls left working, and none of them were attractive. I watched as a heavy girl muddled through a stage set. One man in a ball cap watched. Aaron introduced me to a large man at the bar, still dressed in a suit from the night before, hovering alone over a bottle of tequila.

"This is Bill. He's a bouncer at the Rhino," Aaron said.

"This is Laila. She's a dancer at the Rhino."

"Nice to meet you, Laila." Bill poured us each a shot of tequila. We clinked our glasses together and drank.

"I've got to go talk to some other friends here," Aaron explained before shaking Bill's hand and walking away.

"Take another shot," Bill said as he refilled my glass.

"No thanks. It's been a long night already."

"It wasn't a question. Take the shot."

"I like a man who's man enough to tell me what to do," I said.

"I like a woman who knows how to take orders."

127

I nodded and accepted my shot. Bill poured himself another and drank that too. He talked more to himself than to me, but I listened.

"I can make it so you make over $1000 every night. If you want my help just ask. Don't pretend to like me or play games, you know? You just have to ask."

Clearly, Bill was in the middle of an existential crisis - also known as "Sunday morning in Las Vegas."

"I can only imagine the things you've seen," I said.

"Ten years. Ten fucking years I've been working at the Rhino. I make over $250,000 a year, but I'm a God damned pimp," he growled into his empty glass.

"You're not a pimp."

"I need another shot," Bill said. He poured us both another shot.

"I really shouldn't. I'm driving home in a little while."

"It's 8 a.m. The cops aren't looking for drunk drivers. You're fine."

"That's solid logic."

"I sell women to horny tourists," Bill said.

"I'm sure the $250,000 a year makes it go down easier."

"Money doesn't mean anything after a while," Bill said.

"Money still means something to me. It's nice not being broke for once."

"I have a big boat, and a huge house, and everything I want, but I'm a God damned pimp. I don't know how much longer I can do this." I held up my shot.

"Viva Las Vegas?" I said. We clinked our glasses together.

"Viva Las Vegas." Aaron rejoined us at the bar.

"Hey, we're about to head over to Crazy Horse III. You both in?"

"I'm in," said Bill.

"I didn't drink all of this tequila to go home and pass out. Let's go," I agreed.

At 9 a.m., we reached Crazy Horse III. Our table was full of beautiful women, because Aaron had been collecting strippers from their different workplaces throughout the night – the pied piper of Vegas showgirls. Aaron began intently talking to a lovely, on the clock, blonde stripper with the telltale stomach marks of motherhood.

"Hey! I'm Cherry. How about you?" a sexy mixed girl wearing black lingerie sat down beside me.

"I'm Molly. Nice to meet you."

"Are you a waitress at a club?" she asked me.

"No, I'm a stripper at the Rhino." She looked me up and down, sizing me up.

"I used to work at the Rhino," she said. "I still tell people I'm a Rhino girl when they ask."

"Yeah, it's good there." Cherry and I continued talking, and in the sleepless darkness of the morning, we decided we were friends.

"I'll give men hand jobs for $1000," Cherry confessed. "I have no problem with that at all. What I do is get them all excited until I know they're about to cum, and then I stop and tell them they need to tip me $1000." Cherry laughed.

"They almost always say yes and give me the money. Otherwise, I stop."

"Very nice." I said.

"Let's go to the bathroom together," Cherry said. In the bathroom, I saw the blonde stripper who had danced for Aaron crying.

"Are you okay?" I asked her.

"Yes, I'll be okay," she said. "It's just I love him, and now he's out there with a new girl he's with."

"You love Aaron?" I asked in disbelief. This made blonde stripper number three. That man was a menace.

"We used to be together. We were serious for a while. Then, it didn't work out. I still love him," she said mournfully.

"Well, listen," I told her, "I've met two of his girlfriends, and the one out there is my least favorite of the two. I can tell he loves you – in his way. I saw the way he looked at you. I haven't seen him look at any other girl that way." I watched the woman dry her tears, and Cherry offered her some cocaine to cheer her up, which she refused.

"Thank you. That's good to hear." She smiled. Cherry and I headed back out onto the floor. Cherry trusted me enough now for another confession.

"I'll have sex for money too," she said. "The money you can make is amazing."

"Yeah? How much do you charge?" I asked.

"$1,000 a time," she said.

"Girl, you're underselling yourself. You could make more." I said. Cherry looked confused.

"Do you think so?"

"Absolutely, if you're willing to go all in, then you could be making $30,000 a weekend to fuck the GOP."

"I want to be a madam," Cherry told me. "Start my own business. I'd help set up women with clients. Look at that girl with this broke guy," she said, pointing at the blonde girlfriend now sitting on Aaron's lap. She could be making millions of dollars, but instead she's fucking some loser for free. There are so many women who could be making millions. I could help them."

"I used to joke about being the next Heidi Fleiss. I'll help you. We'll start a business together," I said.

"Are you smart?" Cherry asked me.

"Oh yeah. That's about all I am," I said.

"Good, I need someone smart. I'm street smart, but I'm not book smart."

"I read books. I was in honors in college and everything," I said.

"What did you study?" Cherry asked.

"Strategic communication," I said. "I communicate strategically."

"Every smart pimp I've ever met studied sociology or communication." she said. "You're a smart pimp."

"I'm working on it," I said.

Cherry and I made plans, that haven't come to fruition (yet), to be badass madams, pimping our high-end hoes out to tricks and pocketing their cold hard cash.

There was talk amongst our group of heading back to Aaron's for topless hot tub action, but I'd been working since 8 p.m. the night before, and now it was 11 a.m. the next day. I was exhausted. I said my goodbyes to the group, and headed home to my bed.

SHE LOVES ME, SHE LOVES ME NOT

"I'd see you around the club, and you'd always be walking around smiling," Avalon said, "And I would think, 'This bitch must be new.' Everyone else is pissed off to be there, and you're walking around smiling." My happiness irritated the crap out of Avalon.

"I smile a lot," I said by way of an explanation.

I'd finally made a friend! She was a sexy blonde stripper from Wisconsin, called Avalon, who was living month-to-month in a hotel room down the road from my apartment. She was into yoga, and she was trying to live a life of kindness. She hadn't had the best family life growing up.

"I used to be a bitch," Avalon said. "I had a really bad temper and all, but I'm trying hard now to be a good person."

I wasn't alone anymore! I finally had someone to talk to about my new life dancing. Our first time hanging out together, I wasn't able to shut up for hours. I was finally able to vent everything I'd been thinking to someone who could relate.

"You've just started dancing, I've been doing this for two years. I don't really like talking about it the way you do," Avalon said. "Stripping depresses me."

"I totally understand," I said before continuing my story about the amusing thing that had happened to me the night before at the Rhino.

Avalon and I would go hiking, do yoga, and put in our blonde hair extensions together. We'd talk shop, and she would tell me I give up too easily when a man says *no*. Apparently, when men say *no,* what they're really saying is, "Try harder to get my money."

"Most virtue is a demand for greater seduction."

I'd say stripping wasn't so bad. Avalon would say stripping had sucked all of the life out of her leaving her an anxiety-ridden shell of her former self. I'd stretch luxuriously and proclaim, "Yoga has my ass looking better than ever!" Avalon would say that she'd eaten a bunch of cookies and couldn't work that night because her thighs were too fat, and that she was going to run ten miles the next day to balance out the cookie binge. I'd say that I was a writer, and Avalon would say that she was a writer, then I would go write, and Avalon would go watch television.

"When we go out, let's tell everyone we're lesbian lovers, and we're both yoga instructors," Avalon would say before we went anywhere together.

"All right," I'd agree. Avalon had a long-distance boyfriend in Alabama, but she'd begun to suspect she was a lesbian. When you're a stripper, it becomes hard to tell if you're a lesbian or if you've simply lost all interest in men due to overexposure. Regardless, a large part of our friendship was Avalon pretending that I was her girlfriend. I didn't care; finally having a friend felt good.

**

One day, Avalon and I were sitting in the Champagne room at 10:30 a.m., with a hundred sleepy strippers, eating some awful excuse for breakfast food.

"Girls, listen up!" A bouncer called out. "LEAVE YOUR PURSES IN YOUR LOCKERS. I know you all want to bring your purses with you and have your makeup and everything but don't! You don't need your purse! Every year, girls lose their purses or have them stolen. You're free to take them, but don't come crying to me when you're drunk and someone's stolen your purse, because I'm not going to care! ALSO, DO NOT DRIVE GOLF CARTS WHILE DRUNK! IF YOU CRASH A GOLF CART, YOU WILL PAY FOR THE DAMAGES."

Today was the Spearmint Rhino charity golf tournament, a strip club field trip! In exchange for three free house fees, a $240 value, the girls had the chance to go to a daylong charity golf event. We'd be fed three meals, all of the alcohol we wanted, and if we felt like hustling (optional) we could try and get tips from the golfers. Today was going to be a great day!

A curly brown-haired nymphet with green eyes that radiated mischief, sat down to join Avalon and me. The nymphet sized me up, and ignoring Avalon, asked me my name.

"I'm Molly," I said. "How about you? What's your story?"

"I'm Lady Seda," the nymphet haughtily replied. "I'm going to grad school to be a neuroscientist here in Vegas."

"My story is *Don't Cry, Big Bird.* Big Bird was sad, because he was too big for the children's games. But then, Big Bird met Snuffalupagus. Then, Big Bird was happy, because he had found a friend as big as he was."

"I like that joke." Seda said. "I'm going to steal it from you." Seda and I smiled at each other.

"Thanks, it's one of my favorite pick up lines. It only works on smarter men though. Dumb men are confused by puns. And neuroscience! I'm interested in psychology and philosophy. I've been practicing lucid dreaming, mainly because I sleep so

135

much. Also, I'm a yoga instructor. I was trained over this past winter in Costa Rica."

"Costa Rica? That's so cool." Seda said. "I'm saving up money to go to Spain over the summer. I lived in Europe for a couple of years. I was a high school exchange student in Spain my senior year of high school."

"I was a high school exchange student in Brazil my junior year of high school. I speak Portuguese. Also, I'm a writer. I've been trying to write a screenplay about stripping."

I'd said every good thing I could think of to try and make Seda like me. Avalon bristled beside me. She must have noticed my performance. I might as well have been doing back flips while yelling, "Look at me! Look at me!" I realized the situation was akin to a sexy man ignoring my boyfriend while he blatantly hit on me. I grew concerned for my new genius nymphet's safety.

"This is Avalon," I introduced my lesbian yoga instructor lover to her competition. "She speaks Polish."

"Nice to meet you," Avalon glared.

**

Seda, Avalon, and I danced around to the DJ in our bikinis at the Red Bull tent on the green. Most of the girls were in bikinis, but sometimes, a drunken topless stripper drove by hanging off the back of a golf cart. Another topless stripper taunted men from a dunking booth, while golfers tried to hit balls onto the target that would drop her into the water. Three topless girls held hands and slid down a slip-n-slide together. Jim, the typically intimidating night manager, was running around squirting squealing strippers with a Super Soaker.

"Throw these at the bouncers!" Jim said to me, with a twinkle in his eye, as he placed three small plastic balls in my hands. Then, he ran away laughing as a girl unleashed a torrent of plastic balls in our direction.

Over Red Bull vodkas, Seda recited an impassioned impromptu monologue:

"I see girls who know how to use their power! They are these beautiful goddesses leading the men," Seda swayed, walking backwards, as she beckoned me towards her with one finger, "Straight into the VIP." *Be still my heart.*

"Then, there are girls who buy into this bullshit patriarchal society telling us we should be ashamed of ourselves and our undeniable power, and they act like victims, and they let themselves be used."

"Exactly!" I said.

"I wrote my undergraduate thesis on whether or not prostitution should be legalized. The answer is *yes*. Prostitution needs to be legitimized, because right now, the very act of keeping it illegal is patronizing. Women would be much safer if selling sex was legal and regulated." I walked in close to Seda.

"I've been looking for you. I knew you had to exist, or at least, I really hoped you did," I whispered. Avalon couldn't hear me. Officially, I was in love with a stripper.

**

A few weeks later, Avalon and I were in her hotel room getting ready for the grand opening of Wet Republic pool at MGM where I hoped to meet the extremely talented Kim Kardashian.

"That girl Seda really thinks she's something special. I don't like her," Avalon said.

"Really? I like her a lot. I don't think she's stuck up," I said.

"You can tell she thinks she's better than everyone else. I hate when girls are like that. Don't you?"

"I suppose…"

"I've been in a bad mood lately," Avalon said. "I don't know why."

"We should do more yoga together. Bad moods are nearly impossible if you do enough yoga," I said. Yoga had become my solution to every possible problem and a damn good one at that. Avalon combed through a blonde hair extension before clipping it into the back of her head.

"I've been thinking about this one time, back when I was working selling designer watches, I was dating a guy that I worked with," Avalon said. "I really liked him a lot. Then, he started dating this other girl too, and she was better than me."

"I'm sure she wasn't better than you, Avalon. You're great."

"No, she was better. I was so mad, because this girl was so pretty and smart. I knew she was better than me, and he had to like her more," Avalon stared me down. I stared levelly back with a blank expression.

Avalon suspected I was cheating on her with Seda; she imagined the worst, and she was right. I had secretly been doing yoga with Seda for weeks. In fact, the day before, Seda and I had been doing yoga together in our bikinis in her backyard (complete with a hot tub and pool), when the sprinkler system came on. We were getting drenched, and Seda started to move out of the water.

"Stay," I commanded, and Seda stayed, and we did a vinyassa, under the sprinklers, as the water ran down the curves of our bodies. It was one of the most sensual moments of my life... oh wait, I was writing about Avalon being worried about my fidelity...

Avalon's and my relationship had been based on the fact we were each other's only friend. As summer approached, and everyone came out of hibernation, I started to make new friends.

"Did you want to do yoga together, and then put oil on our hair and face and sit in the steam room tonight?" Avalon asked.

"I would, but I'm going to a pool party at a friend's house. You should come with me. The people there are all young, attractive, and fun," I said.

"No thanks, I'm going to stay in and write, I guess," Avalon said. Every new friend I made distanced me from my yoga instructor-stripper lover. Avalon seethed, and I pretended not to notice. Within a couple of weeks, Avalon had gone from talking about breaking up with her boyfriend and moving in with me so we could start companies together and write books to not returning my texts.

I cared for Avalon, but I was in no state of mind to be in a committed monogamous relationship - especially because I'm straight. My lesbian girlfriend had to go, and go she did. Avalon moved to Alabama to be with her boyfriend.

THE WORST DATE I'VE EVER BEEN ON

"Hey, I'd love to meet up for sushi and then Afrojack at Surrender tonight. Interested? Mike."

I rubbed my hung over eyes and looked at the text I'd just received – it was 1 p.m. – what was this guy doing texting me so early on a Sunday? I didn't remember who Mike was, or what Mike looked like, but at 7 a.m., I remembered there had been a fuzzy shape I'd enjoyed talking with at the Rhino, and I assumed that was Mike. No, of course I didn't want to hang out with Mike. I ignored the text. I looked through my phone to see what actual person I could spend time with that day. Several hours later, when no friends had returned my texts, and I'd become hungry and wanted to eat free sushi, I texted Mike back.

"Yeah, sounds great! I'd love to see you! When and where?"

I walked into the lobby of the Cosmopolitan where I'd agreed to meet Mike. Not knowing what he looked like was a real problem now, and I looked around passively trying to see if anyone was looking back at me.

"There you are, Molly!" a tall good-looking man, with a weak chin and brown eyes, came over and gave me a hug.

"Mike, It's good to see you again! I had so much fun with you last night! Let's get dinner!" We went to sushi at the Cosmopolitan, and Mike told me he lives in LA but also promotes in Las Vegas.

Oh no! I'd accidentally agreed to a date with a promoter. This was going to be bad. The very skill set necessary for being a successful promoter is the exact same skill set necessary for being a complete douche bag.

"Oh that's cool," I said, as I quickly ordered a second glass of wine from the waitress. "How do you enjoy being a promoter?"

"I only promote for fun. I actually have a very large trust fund. My dad is basically the Bill Gates of wine.

"We have so much in common. My dad is basically the Bill Gates of Motown music," I said.

"Yeah, everyone's always impressed by how wealthy my family is. He has a lot of money. He has eight houses, or maybe nine, I can't remember. I'll fly you to LA, and you can go on my yacht with me. We can drink margaritas our in-home chef makes. It's really fun for my friends and me to float our yachts next to each other for parties. You'll like my yacht." I would have bet money borrowed from a psychotic mobster on the threat of death, on this kid being completely full of shit

"I look good on yachts," I said.

He's likely pathological and doesn't even know he's lying anymore, I reasoned, *This is good, because if he thinks he's rich, I won't have to pay to see Afrojack tonight.*

"… We'd met at the Hamptons and became fast friends one summer." I stopped looking for telltale liar body language, and came in for the end of Mike's story about his rich friend.

"The Hamptons are for the lower-income rich," I countered as I swirled my wine around, inserting my nose in the glass to test the bouquet.

"My family only vacations at the resort we built for ourselves on our private tropical island. We only invite our most fabulous friends." He nodded and smiled, because he hadn't heard a word I'd said all night.

"You're so interesting. Everything you say is interesting to me," Mike said. "Girls always try to use me for my money, you know? I want someone to like me for me and not my money."

What? He'd just talked nonstop throughout dinner about how much money his family had and everything his dad owned. The only thing I knew about him was that he was "rich" and now he was saying not to like him for that.

We left dinner and stopped in at Marquee Nightclub in the Cosmopolitan, where he promoted, to see LMFAO before heading to the Encore to hear Afrojack at Surrender Nightclub. The only LMFAO song I knew was Party Rock, and by the millionth time I'd heard it, I'd wanted to water board both members of the group until they promised never to make more music. But Marquee was easily the best part of the date, because Mike got us in for free, we cut the huge line, and he bought me a drink. Mike knew a lot of people at Marquee, and he walked around introducing me to all of them as his girlfriend. As we'd walk away, he'd tell me how the people who'd gotten discounted bottles from him were his best friends.

"Usually, I'd offer to buy the next round on a date, but since you keep saying how rich you are, It'd be pretty strange for me to buy you a drink," I said when I'd finished my first vodka tonic.

"Actually, that would be great if you could get the next round," Mike said.

Wait, what? No. What is happening? I thought he was trying to have sex with me, and if that was really the case, then there's no way I should be paying for my own drinks. It's just wrong! You might as well ask me to tie *myself* up and put *myself* in your trunk.

Please don't misunderstand me; I typically fall in love with young broke artists, and when I go out with them, at the end of the night, we split the check at Denny's, and I treat us both to an ice cream. But if your entire game is to tell me how rich you are, and that by being with you I will be able to enjoy a lot of glamorous free stuff, then you *must* buy all of my drinks. I bought us a round, and as I simmered over how unfair the world can be, Mike grabbed my hand.

"Let me introduce you to LMFAO! I'm really good friends with the one guy. We've hung out a lot, and I helped book them tonight." Mike attempted to dodge LMFAO's bodyguard as he headed for their VIP table, but was stopped.

"I know [DJ team member], can you get his attention for me?" Mike asked the bouncer. The bouncer went to tap [DJ team member] on the shoulder, and pointed over at Mike. [DJ team member] looked directly at Mike, maintained a blank face, and shook his head *no*.

Mike looked as though he'd taken a turtle hit in Super Mario and shrank to half his previous size. Oh my goodness, that was so embarrassing – for me. I felt so bad for myself. LMFAO had dissed me. I felt dirty. I wanted to go home and scrub myself until I felt normal again, if that was even possible now.

"They aren't even good," Mike snarled as he pulled me away. "They only have one song and the rest of their music sucks."

Ah, at least he was humiliated, I thought. *That's nice.* He drew me to stand by a low wall. A group of good-looking club-goers walked over to him, said hello, and thanked him for the table. He introduced me as his girlfriend again. When they walked away, he was smiling as though he'd farted a rainbow.

"Wow, babe," he said, "You must be so impressed by how humble I am! I'm good-looking, rich, and everyone knows me, but I'm still so humble! You must be so impressed!"

"It's not humble to tell people you're humble." I rolled my eyes. Mike's face dropped in total disbelief that he'd failed to impress me. Maybe he hadn't articulated how awesome he was enough yet? Well, the night was still young, maybe if he talked about it some more...

We took a taxi down the strip to Surrender to see Afrojack and Feed Me. I really love these DJs, and I wanted to watch them, but when we were standing in line to get into the club, the date became too much. I decided I couldn't deal with one more story about his fictitious wealth, or how his ex-girlfriend was famous for being on Nip/Tuck. Whatever it was – it was too much. I made up my mind. I quickly yelled I had to go (something about Cinderella and pumpkins), ducked under the velvet rope, and sprinted away in my heels. I was concerned that he was going to chase after me. I paid $15 for a taxi back to the Cosmopolitan, got my car, and drove to Seda's house to recount my gift from the comedy gods.

Mike called me the next day to invite me to lunch and later that night about a pool party he was throwing that weekend. What part of me sprinting away didn't he understand? Another Vegas lesson learned: There's no need to ever be nice to men to get free stuff outside of work. I'd much rather make my own money at the Rhino and then pay for my own sushi.

<u>GAMBLING</u>

Stripping was gambling. I was an independent contractor, not a Rhino employee, and I needed to pay an $80 house fee to the club every time I worked. I'd also tip the mandatory safety valet $5, and the DJ $15. Showing up for work was putting a $100 bet on Molly being able to bank on her feminine wiles. Many nights, this gamble would be enough to stop me going into work. If I didn't feel like a party, if I couldn't do a good job meeting new people and being seductive, then I could leave with less than I came in with – a very real possibility.

Every night, I went to the Rhino, I wanted to win big; I wanted to find my perfect man. I knew he was in the club every single night, somewhere, and it was up to me to meet him and take all of his money. Somewhere, out in the Vegas night, out of all of the drunken belligerent assholes; rich anxiety-ridden men who were too afraid and awkward to talk to women; and broke handsome charmers, somewhere in the midst of the madness, Molly could be found searching for her perfect man.

My perfect man, for the purpose of work, was a man with whom I have great rapport and sincerely enjoy spending my time. A man to whom I am sexually attracted, he doesn't need to be great-looking, just have that je ne sais quoi that gets me going, and he has to have a lot of money he will gladly spend on me. Meeting this man was winning the stripper jackpot, and when I'd hit big, I'd leave smiling, rich, and victorious.

However, you win some, and you lose some. And on some nights, I lost big and, on those nights, I left broke and in tears.

Losing

On my first night back at work after my Costa Rican revival, my game was off. In Costa Rica, I'd had a good cry and dealt with my issues; I was feeling good. The manic post-breakup desire to rage hard and fast and fuck the consequences was all but gone. I was feeling stable for the first time in a long time, and I didn't want stripping to interfere with my newfound bliss. I wanted to do yoga, meditate, eat vegetables, and say *namaste* to all of the world's creatures. I wanted to relish being one with the OM and dance with infinity. I didn't want to dance topless for horny tourists in Sin City. My energy vibrated victim; I was vulnerable, uncomfortable, and a little scared. But as charming as my idealism was, when the rent is due, then the rent is due, and so it sometimes goes.

"Just until I have money saved, then I'll find something else," I rationalized as I plunged tits first back into the darkness of the Rhino. I approached a short chubby man wearing a sloppy business suit and a loose tie.

"How are you doing? My name is Molly," I said. "Let's get a dance."

"My name's Nick. You are gorgeous, Molly. Yeah, let's get a dance."

I walked him over to a chair, took off my bra, and danced for a song.

"Would you like another dance?" I asked.

"Yeah, keep going," Nick said. After finishing my second song, I again asked.

"Would you like another dance?"

"Just keep dancing 'til I tell you to stop."

"Sorry to do this," I timidly apologized, "But could I get the money for those last two dances before this next song? It's $40."

"What, $40 for that? No fucking way! You're trying to rob me."

"Sorry, yeah. Forty is what you owe me," I whimpered. I told you my game was off.

"I don't have that much money."

"There are ATM machines. We can go get some out," I said.

"This is bullshit. I can't believe this," he spat. *My thoughts exactly you piece of shit.* Nick stood up and tried to walk away from me. I followed him and took a hold of his arm.

"What? You're going to follow me now, you whore? Let go of my arm." He yanked his arm away from me.

"You owe me $40," I said, fighting back tears.

"You're not worth that much," he told me. When he realized he was not getting away without paying me, Nick reluctantly pulled out some cash and started slowly counting money out. He handed me a twenty-dollar bill.

"That's twenty," I said. "You still owe me another $20." I watched him very slowly count out ones, as though he was doing me a favor even considering paying me. Then, he dropped the ones on the floor.

I can barely write this over a year later, I'm still so ashamed of myself - *I bent down to pick them up.*

A man who had told me I wasn't worth $40 had thrown one-dollar bills on the floor of a strip club to physically demonstrate his lack of respect and his disdain for me, and I had picked them up. If I'm the type of woman who allows an insecurity-ridden little prick to treat me as though I'm nothing, then he's right, I'm not worth $40.

Amidst the dollar bills he was thumbing through, I spotted a twenty and tried to grab the bill out.

"Hey! Don't try to steal my money, you slut! There are ones on the floor for you." *I hate men. I hate stripping. I hate myself.* Harry, the bouncer who'd given me my tour the first night, walked by me, and I grabbed him.

"This guy owes me $20 for a dance, but he won't give me my money. He's dropping ones on the floor and telling me to pick them up."

Harry shined his light in the man's face and then on the bills on the ground.

"Pick them up," Harry commanded. The little man hesitated.

"Now," Harry elaborated. I don't know what it is, but something about massive bodyguards in black suits, who appear as though they would enjoy nothing more than beating the shit out of drunken tourists, is extremely persuasive. Nick bent to retrieve the ones.

"I can't believe this. I don't deserve this," he whined. He stood, clutching the ones in a pudgy fist.

"Give her the money," Harry said while shining his light on the money. Nick began counting.

"Eleven, twelve, only eight more to go." I helped the bastard add. He begrudgingly handed me the dough and stormed off.

**

Seda had told me repeatedly that I should buy a purse and keep my money and phone with me, because then she'd be able to call me while we were at work, and we could work as a team. Also, Seda explained, robberies were frequent at the Rhino, and the lockers might not always be safe. I ignored her and would periodically deposit money in my locker throughout the night. One night, I was on a lucky streak, and after only two hours, I was up $300. I went to put the money in my locker, and the door was already open, and the locker was empty. All of my stuff was gone.

No, I must be more intoxicated than I thought, and I've forgotten which locker is mine. That makes sense. I looked around the locker room to find where my locker *actually* was. I didn't find it, and the more I stared into that first empty locker, the more I remembered seeing the same *Las Vegas Weekly* magazine sitting on the bottom, when I put my stuff away earlier in the night. All of my stuff had been stolen.

My lock probably hadn't closed all of the way, and someone was able to casually pull it open and quickly grab all of the contents. Luckily, I had almost all of my money on me. At most, the thief had gotten $40 in ones. But they'd also gotten: my smartphone; my driver's license; and my Sheriff's Card, which I needed to work. They had even taken the spandex pants from the blue, white, and yellow uniform I'd had to wear every day when I was 16 and studied at the Brazilian private high school, *Energia*. Those pants were of great sentimental value.

No! My brain refused to believe what logic insisted was true. I went up to the front and told the bouncer about my stolen possessions. The bouncer also suspected I had probably drunk too much and misplaced my locker. He came with me into the locker room to help me find where my locker *actually* was. When we didn't find my locker together, I broke down into tears.

"We need to fill out a report," he told me. Since I'd been left with only lingerie and sparkly high heels, a bouncer handed me an XXL Rhino T-shirt that said:

I'm a Spearmint Rhino Supporter!

I wore the T-shirt as a dress, while I sat on a stool near the back check-in entrance. I don't know exactly what I yelled, but I was furious, and whatever it was, I'm sure that it was something offensive about women who work in the sex industry… Not the best stuff to be shouting next to a line of Vegas strippers waiting to begin their night.

"Hey!" the bouncer yelled at me. "You can get fired for saying something like that. Just be happy you still have a job right now!" I pouted silently on my stool, as I filled out the paperwork. Too distraught to continue my night, I left early, and tipped the back door bouncer $10 to try and smooth things over.

I stood outside waiting for my car to be brought around: crying and owning nothing but glitter heels and lingerie. I glared down at the silhouette of the girl swinging around a pole on my XXL T-shirt turned dress.

"I know it was you that took all of my things, you thieving floozy," I said, accusing that cocky silhouetted good-for-nothing.

The silhouette jumped, spun, and executed a perfect upside down split. She replied in her idiotic Barbie voice:

I'm a Spearmint Rhino Supporter!

**

On a Thursday night, I had already made my house fee back early, and I was in a good mood. I was rewarding myself by taking my time drinking with a good-looking group of Australian men.

"You shouldn't talk to good-looking young guys, they're arrogant and broke. They expect more of your attention for less money. The older guys know you need to be paid for your time," Seda had coached me.

She was right. On one occasion, Avalon had needed to physically pull me away, when I'd become absorbed in a conversation with a brown-haired, blue-eyed, construction worker with a Ganesh tattoo on his forearm. Another night, I'd stopped working after making only $80 profit to talk to a gorgeous chef from San Diego in Vegas with his friends from the Navy for his 30th birthday. A rookie mistake, I have wasted entire nights at work letting pretty eyes and a nice smile distract me from my pursuit of making money. This was, perhaps, going to be one of those nights, but I had blind faith that the gorgeous blond man I was giggling at would stop buying me drinks any time now and start buying hour-long VIP dances.

"Does he actually have any money, or is your buddy playing me?" I asked the brown-haired friend.

"He has money. He has more money than he knows what do with." That sounded promising, but every man in Vegas lies to every woman in Vegas saying they're the rich CEO of something, or a venture capitalist, or they've inherited a large trust fund. Everything could have been a lie, but the blond had the swagger of a kid who'd never had to work for his money but felt he'd earned it regardless. *Let's see if I can get Mr. Pretty to pay this month's rent.*

Unfortunately, the brown-haired friend decided he liked me too. The two men began competing for my attention. When two men in the same group are interested in one stripper, it's important to pick between the two of them very quickly. If I took too long to commit to a man, then he might get offended that I didn't think he was special enough to have garnered all of my attention.

151

Unfortunately, if I picked incorrectly, then I'd be stuck talking to the "not a strip club kind of guy," the male equivalent of the "not that kind of a girl," while I'd watch the friend, who could have been mine, take another stripper into the VIP. I'd already placed my bet with the blond friend, but the brown-haired friend said, "Let's go to VIP. I want a dance with you."

Great. If the cute blond guy is going to play hard-to-get, I'll go with his less attractive but easier friend - no problem. I walked with brown-haired "Steve" over to the VIP.

"It'll be $200 to the lady up front," the bouncer told Steve, "And then you need to buy two drinks once you're inside. Is it going to be cash or credit?"

"Oh, I hadn't wanted to spend that much money," Steve said.

Damn it, Steve! Not only did I not get money from Steve, but he'd also ruined the time I'd spent with his blond friend. I hurried back to the blond to pretend I hadn't gone away with his friend after all. The blond and I started talking where we'd left off, but Steve hadn't finished ruining my night yet. Steve liked me too much to let his friend take me to the VIP room he couldn't afford. He was determined to cock block my game.

"Let's get a dance on the floor," Steve said. "How much?"

"Twenty."

"All right, yeah, let's get one of those," Steve said. I danced a song for Steve. When the song ended, I put my bra back on, and Steve pulled out a hundred-dollar bill.

"Can you make change for this?" Steve asked.

"Probably," I said. "Let me check in my purse." I found $60, which I handed to Steve, before continuing to dig through my bag for the last $20. While I was looking in my bag, Steve pocketed my $60. I looked up.

"Can I get that hundred?" I asked.

"What do you mean $100? I only owe you $20," Steve said.

"No, I gave you $60 already. You need to give me that hundred."

"You didn't give me any money," Steve said.

"Yes, I did," I said, starting to doubt myself. "Didn't I?"

Steve's serious expression broke, and he laughed at his prank.

"Yes, you did give me money!" he admitted excitedly. I smiled at him and laughed.

"I knew it. Give me that hundred then!" Steve stopped smiling. I could see in his eyes that in his drunken state this game of toying with the stripper was too much fun to give up. I watched him shrink down to the size of a first grade boy looking to push me in the dirt.

"You didn't give me any money," he said. This wasn't good. Probably, the right choice would have been to ignore him and hope he got bored and returned my money, but what if that didn't work and he was so drunk he forgot about me and wandered away?

"You stole my money," I said. "You need to give me my money back. You stole my money," I repeated over and over again in disbelief.

"No, I didn't," Steve said. "I have plenty of money. You're a liar. Why would I steal your money?" I turned to the blond friend for help.

"Please, help me. Your friend took my money!" I said. The blond, confused, stared silently to see what was happening. Steve took off into the club, leaving me by his blond friend. Other men from his group came over.

"Help me find your friend," I said. "He stole $60 from me!" All four men stared at me as though I was something they'd accidentally stepped in.

"Why the hell would he steal from you? Steve has plenty of money. Steve doesn't need *your* money." Their eyes radiated disgust as they imagined the injustice of Steve being slandered by a lying Vegas stripper.

Having noticed my mounting hysteria, suddenly three bouncers were by my side asking me what had happened (likely to preemptively prevent me from hitting someone). I recounted my story.

"She's not lying. One of you stole this girl's money and needs to give it back," a large black bouncer announced clearly and loudly to the now small-looking Australian men.

"You need to tell me exactly what happened," a bouncer said as he pulled me aside. As I began to recount my tale of woe once more, Steve returned and quickly "found" my $60 in his pocket. I never did get the $20 for the lap dance. The Australians left the club immediately. I hugged all of the bouncers. They hugged me back, and I felt as though they were my friends, protecting me from men who wanted to hurt me. I resolved to tip more, because I suddenly loved them all very much.

"Thank you for believing me," I said to them. "I needed that."

GIRLS NIGHT OUT

"LICK MY PUSSY!" Tiffany, the gorgeous blonde who'd had the threesome with my boyfriend, yelled as we left a college bar in downtown Columbus, Ohio. The men she yelled at looked confused.

"Did I stutter, you ugly shits? I SAID, 'LICK MY PUSSY!'" Tiffany screamed. I watched the two guys get worried and start to walk quickly towards their car. They were afraid of what this crazy bitch might do to them.

"Where are you going? My pussy needs to be licked! Come back here and LICK MY PUSSY!" Tiffany jerked both hands downward towards her beautiful glittery pelvis. The men couldn't get away from this petite Miss America contestant fast enough.

Tiffany, Christina, and I laughed hysterically. We'd left the college bar moments before and the jackasses Tiffany had frightened away had yelled the typical machismo bullshit at us.

"Hey baby, suck my dick!"

"Hey sexy, how are you doing?"

"Hey gorgeous, where you going? I'll show you a good time." Pretty standard. It's what I hear every day walking down the street.

155

But this was the first night in my entire life they were not getting away with making me feel uncomfortable, frightened, and small.

"Don't let the bastards grind you down."

"Holy shit," I thought, "*They're* running from *me!*"

I was 21 - a senior in college. Since I was 16 living in Brazil: I've had men follow, even chase, me through the streets; I've watched my drinks closely to make sure no one puts anything in them; I've never walked alone at night; and I will not, and I mean never, get into your fucking car. Finally, for the first time in my life, I didn't feel like the potential victim.

Well, I decided, *this is how it's going to be from now on. No more weak, scared, little girl crap. No more always being on the defense hoping that no one decides to hurt me. Try and touch me; I'll kick you in the balls and pepper spray you while you're down.*

When strippers talk about power and control this is what we mean. In the strip club, the men are women, and the women are men. I'm not the prey in the strip club – the men are. You can't take advantage of me in the strip club; you can only come to a mutually beneficial agreement with me where you give me your money, and I give you blue balls. You can't attack me in the strip club; a bouncer will kick you out and have you arrested. I'm cool with you lying to me in the strip club; I promise you, I've lied to you at least ten times by now.

I felt liberated going into work. I wasn't a pretty young thing men thought they could take advantage of; I was a *fucking stripper* - most likely an unstable, drug-addled, thieving whore. I was not to be trusted. Men were wary of my intentions. Men were afraid *I* was going to take advantage of *them*. I had all of the power. It felt great, and if you're looking for an apology, or for me to feel ashamed of myself, don't hold your breath.

SALES ADVICE FROM A LAS VEGAS STRIPPER

1) The ABCs - Always Be Closing

Anyone can sell, but can you close? A potential mistake is to spend a lot of time building rapport with a customer and then, when it's time, being unable to pull the trigger on the sale. When I first began working at the Rhino, I'd spend my entire night with a couple of men.

"I don't plan on buying a dance," they'd tell me.

"That's okay. I'm enjoying talking to you!" I'd answer, and bless my little heart, I'd mean it too. In the beginning, when Molly moved to Las Vegas, a night making $200 felt like winning, and I was all but guaranteed to make that, therefore I was always at ease, and I enjoyed myself partying and meeting new people. More often than not, after an hour of talking with me, the men who had said they didn't want a dance would change their tunes and spend hundreds on me in the VIP.

But then, I had several nights in a row where this didn't work. The men didn't change their minds. I'd woken up at 1 a.m., jet lagged myself, drank body destroying liquor, and wasted hours of work time talking to some random men I'd never see again, and for my troubles, I'd left with nothing but a hangover.

When I'd only given myself a night or two to make rent, $200 quickly stopped feeling like winning. I had to learn to target. I had to learn to close.

I began to size the men up. Did they look as though they had money? Was this man going to be worth a 20-minute time investment? Was there going to be a pay off, or was I wasting my time on a man who talked big but spent small? If I sized a man up incorrectly, I could end up wasting my time with no pay off, or alternatively, I could leave a man too early only to see him bring the next girl who was more patient into the VIP for the rest of the night.

First, I'd build rapport, make the men feel special, not like a meal ticket, then, when I'd see their eyes change, they'd look friendlier, softer, more trusting, then I'd know I had them ready to buy; I'd go in for the sale.

"We have such awesome rapport! We're definitely going to the VIP together." There wasn't time to be wasted. Stripping wasn't for fun; stripping wasn't to meet a *nice* man to love me and take care of me; stripping was for money. If I was rejected, at least I was rejected quickly, without too much opportunity cost. Then, it's up and on to the next. Repeat as necessary until rent is paid.

2) Don't ask. Do tell.

When I first started dancing, I'd ask, "Would you like to get a lap dance?" This unfortunate word choice allows a man to spend valuable time thinking about if he'd like to give me money. I was giving him a 50-50 choice.

I might as well have been asking, "Would you like to reject me?" I was foolishly putting his will above mine, his decision above mine, and my pockets suffered for my timidity.

"We're getting a dance next song." Period. Not a question but a command. With this phrasing, I have told the man we're getting a dance, and it's not a 50-50 choice. Now, to reject me, his willpower must be stronger than mine, and not too many drunken horny tourists have stronger willpower than a money-hungry lingerie-clad hussy counting down the men 'til morning Buffy the Vampire Slayer watching time.

3) Giving is a trick for getting.

When I was living in Brazil, a man came up to me in the street.

"No, I don't want to buy anything," I told him before he could speak.

"No, I'm not selling. I want to give you something! I saw you walking, and you're simply so beautiful. I want to make you a beautiful flower." *Flattery will get you everywhere – go on.* I watched the man make a flower out of a pair of pliers and some wire.

"For you, beautiful girl!" he handed me the little flower.

"Thank you," I said. "It's lovely."

"You're welcome. Would you like to buy a bracelet? They're only $5." *I've been bamboozled.* I sighed.

"Yes, of course, I'll buy a bracelet."

I left annoyed at my own gullibility with a poorly crafted bit of leather strapped on my wrist.

The same technique worked in the strip club. I started to carry throat lozenges and cigarettes around with me in my little glitter purse.

"Here, let me light that for you."

"I'm going to have a throat lozenge. Would you like one too?"

Once the men had accepted a small kindness, they became much more likely to agree to give me money. At that point, to say *no* was not only a battle of wills, but honestly, a bit rude. I had been so nice after all.

4) Let's take some shots!

Men would offer to buy me drinks instead of getting a dance. This was annoying, because I didn't want to drink; I wanted to make money. But I'd agree and suggest we take shots together. Then, when the drinks came, I'd take a little of the shot, cover my mouth as though I was going to throw up, then explain I really wasn't able to drink the whole shot after all and that the customer should finish the drink for me. As I explained earlier, I like my men as drunk as possible.

5) Yes, Yes, Yes!

One of my all-time favorite sales techniques was getting the customer to say *yes* three times. The questions don't matter, only that the answer is *yes*. Humans love patterns, and once a pattern of *yes* is established, it takes a lot of effort to say *no.*

"Are you having fun in Las Vegas?"

"Yes."

"Have you been drinking ever since your flight landed?"

"Yes."

"Do you like boobs?"

"Yes!"

"Let's go to the VIP right now!"

"Yes!"

6) Peacocking: not only for guys who can't get laid without the help of a book anymore.

There's a book, *The Mystery Method,* written by a nerd who, through years of observing Alpha males at bars, as well as studying human psychology and courtship, was able to extract a set of rules allowing hopeless men to have sex with women they meet at bars. *The Mystery Method* made such a splash on the dating scene that author Neil Strauss wrote a best-selling novel, *The Game,* about learning to become a PUA (for those too busy getting laid to have heard this term, it stands for "pickup artist").

Unfortunately for devotees of The Mystery Method, women can read too (who knew?), therefore many of us already know the signs to spot a man looking to con us with the *Mystery Method*. However, as much as I hate to admit this, Mystery got it right. Learn, internalize, and make your own his methods; and you truly will have your pick of the drunken, insecure, bar girls. However, to master that level of communication skills takes a degree of social competence the target market of the book clearly lacks which, perhaps, limits its effectiveness.

The Mystery Method is chock-full of great advice. Advice I have successfully used to make money off of the same types of men who would have happily used it to make me believe they liked and respected me in order to have sex with me: smiling a lot, approaching your target within three seconds of making eye contact (incredibly important), setting time limits to your interactions to create a sense of urgency, creating love-triangles to create jealousy in your target, and my favorite, and most oft used, peacocking.

Peacocking is wearing an outlandish outfit or accessory in order to bring more attention to yourself and, if you have the bravado to match your crazy, raise your social value. Strippers are the masters of peacocking. Walking into a strip club is like walking into a rave. (Or is walking into a rave like walking into a strip club?)

Peacocking gives your target something to say to you:

"I like your smiley face T-shirt. Is that a bullet hole in its head?"

"Your headband is stupid, and I don't like it."

"Why would you wear such silly fuzzy boots?"

All of these statements are indicators of interest (IOIs in PUA lingo), and they mean that I can get money off of the guy. Also, my headband is awesome; don't hate.

7) Be drunk and horny.

I talk a lot of bullshit. Forgive me, it was my job for a long time, but there's just no substitute in strip club sales for good old-fashioned drunken horniness.

There was a study done (the validity of which is questionable) where researchers asked strippers to record their tips from lap dances over a period of time. On average, the girls made $70 an hour while ovulating, $35 while menstruating, and $50 in between. The research hypothesized pheromone levels changed throughout the month, and men responded to the increased fertility, slight changes in appearance, and subtle shifts in the behavior of the dancers. By "subtle shifts in behavior of the dancers," scientists meant strippers were *actually* horny for once instead of the weekly drudgery we try to pass off as a fun carefree seduction.

To help increase the world's scientific knowledge, I can tell you that when I'm not actually horny, and I haven't been drinking, this is the sales pitch:

"Let's get a dance."

"Why should I?" The man retorts, threatening my spending cash.

"Because it'd be fun? And I need to pay rent. You'd be a Good Samaritan if you bought a dance... and... because I like you... I guess?"

"Eh, I don't know..."

When I'm actually horny this is the sales pitch:

"Let's get a dance." I massage the man's inner thigh. I smile, maintaining eye contact, and raising an eyebrow. Then, I lick my lips, bite my lower lip, make eye contact, and quickly look away, as though I'm shy.

"Why?" the man says again, threatening my spending cash.

"Because you're gorgeous and interesting, and because I can't wait to get back there with you and have some real fun. Let's go!" By this time, I've climbed on the man's lap and am giving him an impromptu back massage.

"Let me get some more money from the ATM first. How much did you say an hour was?"

A big thanks from my wallet goes out to alcohol, the film Boiler Room (ABC), The Mystery Method, Psychologist Geoffrey Miller and colleagues, and a college marketing lecture that explained sincerity is the key to sales:

Sincerity: once you can fake that, you've got it made.

CAPTAIN SAVE A BITCH

"Have you heard the term Captain Save a Bitch?" I asked Lady Seda.

"No, what is it?"

"Captain Save a Bitch is the name we call those super heroes of real life who try to save us from our sinful lives at the strip club."

"Good, those guys needed a name," Seda said. "The other night I had some guy tell me, 'You should come back to Denver with me, I'll pay for everything. All you have to do is take care of my house, and love me for me.'" Seda and I laughed.

"I was thinking, wow, you really underestimate me." Seda shook her head good-naturedly before returning to her reading on the cerebral cortex.

**

One night, early on in my life as a Vegas stripper, before I knew better than to talk too much about myself, I got in an intense conversation with a rich, young, and very handsome Mexican man - one with a nice, German, last name. I have no idea what I said, but whatever it was played on this well-dressed man's heart strings.

"You deserve better than this," he cried passionately.

"No," I tried to explain. "I'm fine. I'm building a life for myself. I have a plan. This is all temporary. You don't need to worry about me."

"No!" Mexican Captain Save a Bitch wept - heartbroken. He was a compassionate guy who couldn't handle the injustice of a world where the girl he wanted to have sex with, then never speak to again, needed to work twelve hours a week in order to sleep in and buy organic groceries at farmer's markets.

"It's not fair!"

"There, there," I consoled, "I'm happy and healthy, I promise. Want to go to the VIP room for an hour?" Hell, it was still worth a shot, right?

"I don't want to give you money here. Come back with me to my hotel room, and we can be together, and I will give you money."

"Sorry, I don't have sex for money."

"How about for fun?"

"Definitely not for fun."

"All right." Captain Save a Bitch sighed, stood up, and wandered off into the club in search of another stripper to save/have sex with.

**

Look guys, I know it's hard to pick one or the other, but you can either try to save a wretch like me OR fuck a wretch like me. YOU CANNOT DO BOTH. You can either try to have random, irresponsible, nameless sex in Las Vegas with me, OR encourage me to return to school so I can learn to type, cut hair, or whatever. You can either offer me money to suck your dick, OR, and this is a big OR, you can try and save my soul. YOU CANNOT DO BOTH. On behalf of jaded cynical strippers everywhere, I need to write this again: YOU CANNOT DO BOTH. If you're morally opposed to what I'm doing, DON'T COME TO MY WORK. This will completely solve your moral dilemma and save you a lot of energy trying to get me to quit my job and have free sex with you.

* *

"I just can't stand to see you doing this," a hundred-thousandaire from New York City said as I bent over in front of him in the VIP and shook my butt in his face. I rolled my eyes, as I looked at my feet and thought about what color to next paint my toenails. I stood and turned back around. I straddled him and kept one foot on the ground – standard procedure.

"Nah, it's really a pretty good deal," I explained. "I'm a writer. I have all week to write and do yoga, and then two nights a week I dance here, and the money I make is enough to pay for everything I want."

"I feel so terrible to see you wasting your life like this! I really like you. You could be so much more!" He cried out from between my breasts.

"I'm about one hundred pages into the book I'm writing, and I've used the money I've made dancing to become a certified yoga instructor. I'm working now to save up money, and then I'm done dancing, and I'm moving to LA to work on film projects with other artists."

"I care about you! You're doing this to yourself with no plan or way out. It makes me so sad… Can I suck on your toes? I have a thing with feet." In hindsight, I'm fairly positive this was illegal (this wasn't an issue that had been covered in my orientation), but honestly, I couldn't think of anything I wanted more than this rich condescending prick to suckle my unwashed yoga feet. I removed one glittery heel and presented Captain Save a Bitch with my foot. I watched, pleased, as he inserted all of my toes into his mouth. *That is disgusting. I know where that foot's been…* As he removed my foot from his mouth, I decided I'd paint my toenails red next. I started dancing again to hopefully keep the bouncer from noticing the (probably) illegal foot fetish in action.

"Would you come visit me if I flew you to New York City? I have a really great place for you to stay," he said.

"No, I'm not going to New York City to visit you."

"Why not?" he asked.

"Because you're a pathetic loser who doesn't listen. I would never have sex with you. I think you're revolting. Even for a free trip to New York City, having sex with you is not worth it to me." I stuck my foot back in front of his face; all of the little piggily-wigglies wiggling about looked so tempting. How could masochistic Captain Save a Bitch resist something so beautifully degrading?

"Put my foot in your mouth again," I said. He did. What can I say? Captain Save a Bitch never fails to bring out the sadist in me.

MY WING WOMAN – LADY SEDA

Most strippers, myself included, had a handful of dancer friends at the club, and we worked with each other as teams; a good wing woman was an invaluable asset. But after those first few dancer friends were made, none of the strippers talked to one another. This wasn't due to hostility. I'd always felt Rhino girls, though intimidating and, at times, completely terrifying, were courteous, respectful, and had the sense to at least pretend to be nice. If ever a girl accidentally started talking to my man while I was away, when I returned, with few exceptions, the girl would apologize and leave me to try my luck with the guy. On a good night, I didn't have any reason to notice the other women working at the Rhino.

I tried to work with all of my friends at some point, but our styles conflicted. Avalon worked the room like the luxury-goods saleswoman she'd been in her Rolex sales days. Avalon made money through tenacity. A man would have to shove her off his lap to get her to leave without her first scoring at least one floor dance. Carmen, a friend straight out of Portland's Suicide Girls, sported a potent mix of fake black-rimmed glasses, a torso full of tattoos, and a sweetheart attitude that kept her consistently besting me in sales. She was often grabbed by an admirer on the floor and would have them convinced she was their new best friend for life before leaving with all of their money to go home and cuddle with her husband. Avalon was too forceful and Carmen was too laid back for us to successfully combine efforts. Enter lovely Lady Seda.

Seda had become my partner-in-crime in every sense of the word.

We'd buy each other presents on our frequent vacations out of Vegas. Lady Seda brought me back a small elephant statue, a Ganesh, from her winter in India with a card that read, "Giving a Ganesh is said to be auspicious, so I thought it would be perfect for this beautiful writer I know. Let me know if it's true."

I brought her back a yin-yang necklace from the Ohio music festival Summer Dance.

"To help us find balance," I said. Seda and I were constantly striving to find balance.

"Healthy eating, daily yoga, a determined mental attitude, and getting a lot of money off of wasted men on weekends is the key to success," I'd tell her while she worked on homework, and I wrote a blog post about what had happened to me that day in the Las Vegas Athletic Clubs steam room.

In the Rhino, Seda and I were an unstoppable duo, our seduction styles synched perfectly.

"Two little curly-haired girls with big brains, real breasts, and a lot of energy," was how Seda explained our success.

"Two young women with the world at their feet. There doesn't seem to be a limit to anything you can do," my visiting Australian musician friend said, while relaxing by the pool on a Wednesday afternoon with Seda and me.

At work, we'd dance around the room, drinking, and having a great time together – a girl's night out. We'd sit with men and gang up our efforts. I'd talk about how great Lady Seda was and she'd go on about how flexible I am. We'd play off of each other.

"Let's go to the VIP," I told the middle-aged British men we'd been drinking with at the bar.

"I don't know…" one man started to say.

"Of course we're all going to the VIP together! We've spent enough time talking, and we're all having such a good time. They're obviously going to get dances," Seda explained to silly little me. Unable to resist our combined willpower, we took their hands and walked them to the Champagne Room.

"Do you have a friend exactly like you?" an envious man's friend asked me one night.

"Actually, yes, you're going to love her." I told him before heading into the darkness to find Lady Seda. The man and his friend took us both back to the VIP where we sat in adjoining booths.

"She's incredibly smart," I told my man as I danced topless in front of him. "She's in graduate school for neuroscience."

"She's a great writer," I heard Lady Seda, topless next to me, saying to her man as she sipped champagne.

Seda and I created our reality together. We lived in a world where famous seductresses and courtesans were the epitome of power, and we looked down on any society that constrained women and had the balls to call them subservient. Whether stripping was degrading, if we were being used, was not our question. Our question was how to most effectively use the undeniable power of our youth and beauty to help create the world we wanted to live in.

When I told men I was a stripper, I was met with three responses: barely veiled disgust (or sometimes even anger) over

170

my lack of shame; neutrality or disappointment, saying stripping seemed like good money; but, most often, my confession was met with envy.

"I wish I had tits. I could have free time to work on my painting instead of working at a coffee shop 50-hours a week," said my high school boyfriend, and long-term friend, living in New York City.

"When I found out you were stripping, I wasn't repulsed, I was jealous. There's a reason women strip; stripping is better than working! I would strip too - if I could," a college friend paying off his $70,000 in student loans admitted.

"If I had breasts, I'd be running a small country by now," said a handsome Israeli friend at the top of the real estate game in San Francisco.

Was this attitude unexpected? Wasn't I made to believe stripping would ruin my chances of ever finding a decent man? Hadn't I been told I'd be shunned from respectable society? The opposite had proven true.

The Church's venomous conviction that women are evil seductresses; the men who drape their women in shapeless black coffins; the defamations leveled against women who would dare lower themselves to use their sexuality for pleasure or to gain an advantage - these all existed for me in a new light.

Is female sexuality truly so powerful that the conditioned constraints of "religion" and "morality" are necessary to keep it under control?

REGULARS

When I talk about being a stripper, it's from the perspective of a novice. In some ways, I became one of the best strippers, but in a lot of ways, I never progressed my game to the level of expert. I was willing to pretend to like a man for a night, but that's the longest I ever bothered to pretend to like anyone. An expert-level stripper develops a Rolodex of regulars.

I sat by the pool with Daria, Seda's roommate, in school for her MBA. Daria was lovely, married, brilliant, and sarcastic. A giantess of a woman, over 6-feet, her husband towered over her at 6'9." Her husband was a jolly giant of a man. Laid back and handsome, he could typically be found building or fixing something around the house. Daria had been a dancer for 11 years and had better stripper skills than I will ever have.

"My regular needs to leave town now," Daria said. "It was nice at first because I'd go into the club and sit in the back smoking hookah with him, and he'd give me money, and he takes me and Seda out to really nice five-star dinners, but I'm getting sick of it. Every night he wants to take us out for dinner. My husband is getting annoyed."

"I don't think I could have a regular," I said. "I don't mind pretending to like someone for the night, but pretending to like them long-term creeps me out. I'm afraid they'd kill me or something."

"I make sure they're mentally stable," Daria said. "I've gotten probably $30,000 worth of jewelry, a bunch of clothes, my motorcycle, and my truck from men. They all want to feel as though they're helping in some way."

"That's incredible."

"It was really due to laziness. I moved to Vegas and decided I wanted to find someone to buy me a truck, and I did. Then I decided I wanted men to mail me money, and they did. Whenever men say something like, "I can't believe I met you at the strip club, that's a really good sign."

**

In Daria and Seda's house in Henderson, one of two nice Vegas suburbs, the three of us could usually be found on the sofa watching Maury.

"That guy is definitely not the baby's daddy," Seda said. "He knows it too. Look at his eyes." We were experts in determining baby's daddies.

One day, an episode on out-of-control teenage girls was on.

"I went on Maury once for being an out-of-control teenager," I said.

"Seriously?" Seda and Daria asked in unison.

"No, come on guys," I said.

"How were we to know?" Seda scrunched her face.

"Yeah, it definitely seemed likely," said Daria, returning her attention to the thread on her ever-present needlepoint.

"Can you tell what this is yet?" Daria asked, showing me her needlepoint of three butterflies.

"Yeah," I said, "A dragon."

"What?" Daria said, upset. "You really can't tell these are butterflies?"

"Sorry, I see a dragon."

**

"But, I mean, I feel as though I know you," I said to Daria out by the pool. "You're not sleeping with the regulars, are you?" Daria laughed.

"The last thing you want to do is sleep with your regulars. You don't get free stuff by sleeping with people. Not in the long run. You get it by maintaining a relationship, letting them into parts of your life, and retaining enough mystery to stay interesting. You get the money by embodying their perfect woman. If you do it correctly, no other woman will ever be able to live up to what you've created."

"Doesn't having regulars get hard, though?" I asked. "Not sleeping with them? I feel they'd always be trying to have sex."

"I make it very clear our relationship is not going to be sexual," Daria said. "If they ignore me, and repeatedly try to sleep with me, then I stop seeing them."

I've got to confess, the appeal of staying out at VIP tables, and having seven-course meals, sounded a lot better than getting to know endless new men every weekend. Having the same conversation over, and over, and over, until I wanted to scream, only to lose that time invested at the end of the night was bad business. Maybe, I should make a business card and start building a client base?

Call Molly: Yoga Instructor, Stripper, Intelligent... But Not Smarter Than You

Of the strippers who don't go the Rolodex route, but instead make their money in the club, I wasn't one of the top hustlers either. I couldn't have scored one of the permanent lockers after my stint in the darkness. To get a permanent locker at the Rhino, you needed to have worked at least three nights a week for a year (or be in good with management), and I'd typically work one or two nights a week, and I'd skip weeks or months at a time. Because of my laziness, my bank account hovered around zero. Some girls were responsible and treated the Rhino as a normal job. They were able to provide for children and build homes. Often, the only time I'd bother to work was when rent was due. For most of Molly's Vegas vacation, I treated the Rhino as an ATM machine – only frequented when cash money was necessary immediately.

I wasn't at the top of the Vegas stripper heap by a long shot. I usually worked five hours before I left early. Sometimes, I'd tip the bouncers and DJ really well, and sometimes I wouldn't. Whether or not I tipped big never mattered, because by the next time I went into the Rhino, my generosity (or frugality) was forgotten. I never tipped enough to get on lists or get favors. I still had problems closing – my timing was frequently off – either too soon or too late – a moment lost. I couldn't garner favor from the management, or get out of trouble if I got myself into it, and when they took down the sign up sheets for promotions and started asking girls, I was never asked to go.

Despite these shortcomings, I consider myself to have been a successful Las Vegas stripper. I made wonderful friends, I used and abused my ample free time, and I was never put in jail for any reason – not even once. Other than, and including, all of the awful parts, I lived a really great life in Las Vegas. I wouldn't change my two years of stripping, with all of the lying, heartache, hustling, partying, mistakes, and discoveries, for any other experience. I had a terribly wonderful time becoming *The Yoga Stripper*. She's a woman I'm incredibly proud to be.

OLD WHORES DON'T DO MUCH GIGGLING

I walked into the VIP room at 3 a.m. with a lawyer from Miami, and to the right Jasmine, a smiling, topless, Indonesian girl, sat on a man's lap.

"Molly, how are you!" Jasmine squealed.

"Great!" I leaned over the man Jasmine sat on and went in for the hug. I pressed my lingerie-clad breasts against Jasmine's naked chest.

"You look beautiful," Jasmine smiled.

"You too! Always great to see you."

I'd go into the VIP room and there would be Seda, Avalon, or any of my work friends, and we'd enthusiastically say hello, topless, from the laps of our men. It was a great bonding experience. Shared VIP time brought my friendships to a welcome and zany new level.

"I went to Jasmine's wedding," I told the lawyer, as we sat down.

"She had a small wedding at Mandalay Bay. The bride's side was made up of nine Rhino strippers and her Indonesian parents who couldn't speak any English."

"That doesn't even sound real," the lawyer said.

"I know. That's why I love Las Vegas."

**

"Does your conscious bother you? Now tell the truth." The music came through the speakers. Seda and I froze over sipping our drinks. We made heavy eye contact across the table at Blue Martini where we were enjoying Ladies Night Wednesday. Suddenly, the lyrics of *Sweet Home Alabama* felt interrogative.

I'd begun to feel the way I imagined rich and famous men must feel when they decide to start buying whores instead of getting sex from the thousands of ready and willing women dying to sleep with them.

Like those famous men, I was tired of having to lie to get what I wanted.

Even when I had genuine rapport with a man and was enjoying our conversation, all I was thinking was, "Cha-ching! I'll get more money from him if he likes me."

I wished men would still give me their money, if I told them the truth.

"Do you really like me?"

"No, of course not. I don't even know what your face looks like, and I'm looking at it right now. I'd like to show you my breasts in exchange for money, and then I'd like to never have to speak to you again. Right now, I'm fantasizing about my bed, and I'm deciding what I'm going to watch when I get home. I also, against my better judgment, might get a veggie works burrito from Del Taco."

There was no way around the truth; I was tired of chasing rich tail around Las Vegas.

Every man, one after the next, needed to be convinced he stood out from the rest. But no one ever stood out anymore. Every man at the Rhino was equally meaningless. I was ready to move out of Las Vegas and onto my next life.

When I first arrived in Las Vegas, I had dinner with a group that included a 40-something-year-old stripper who'd flown in for the weekend to try and make a quick couple thousand before returning home to her husband and children in Florida.

"I had a threesome with two guys on roller skates before," she told the group. When one of the guys made a joke about how they should all go skating together, she clarified, "I'm married and faithful. I'm actually very boring sexually."

I told her I was going to start stripping that next week – a naive, bushy tailed, young scout telling the weary old pro about how naughty I was planning on being.

"Stripping takes a lot of strength," the jaded mother told me. "You have to be very strong mentally. But if you can handle it, stripping is good money." My first months, I'd think about her saying that and laugh.

"Mentally strong to party in Vegas and have more money than I'd ever seen in my life? Please, stripping is the most fun I've ever had!"

But, as always seems to happen, I've been humbled by the dirty truth of life. Stripping is one hell of a job. It's fast money, and if you have game, stripping can be great money. But the money is by no means easy money. On my way out, I knew she was right; to strip you need to be mentally strong, or it can quickly become a very slippery slope.

After two years at the Rhino, having made my living by approaching strangers in heels and lingerie, sliding onto their laps, and attempting, as quickly as possible, to make them like me enough to give me hundreds of dollars, most social interactions failed to challenge or excite me anymore. For months at a time, I wouldn't go to a normal nightclub but only to work at the Rhino. I'd grown so accustomed to being the aggressor, to having men look quickly down and away when I attempted to make eye contact with them, to being waved away, and rejected, and told, "Sorry, you're not my type. I like Asians," that going to a normal nightclub had become a joke.

As unnatural as a strip club feels to men, suddenly having hundreds of beautiful women laughing at all of your dumb jokes and telling you how great you are, that's how unnatural the real world now felt to me. I'd developed pickup skills no girl should ever have. At a normal club, if I walked alone to the bathroom, I had at least five men try to talk to me, or tell me how beautiful I am, or offer to buy me a drink, only to be insulted by some of the tactics the men would try on me. Their pick up skills were nothing compared to mine. I could teach these boys some things. *Maybe after they're done with their sales pitch on why I should sleep with them, I'll give them a helpful critique of what they're doing wrong? Well, I'll let them buy me a drink first, and then I'll give the helpful critique.*

I'd improved my social skills to beat Vegas' most audacious beauties, and finally, even sitting on laps in lingerie failed to get my heart racing – same old, same old. I needed a new drug. My tolerance to fear had risen too high.

I began taking improv comedy classes. Performers are the perfect friends for strippers, because they're also willing to do practically anything on stage for money and admiration. I'd get up on stage at improv and attempt to create a scene from scratch. Improv reminded me of a nightmare I constantly have where I'm suddenly the star of a play I'd never rehearsed. On stage, I could make people laugh, make them happy, make them think, and I didn't even need to look at them. I love improv (almost) as much as I love yoga – another new passion. How lucky can one girl get?

Strangely enough, stripping in Vegas had the opposite effect you might expect on my partying ways. Stripping made me into a homebody. A few weeks before I moved away from Las Vegas, Seda was sitting beside me finding citations for a research paper, and Daria was working on a new needlepoint of a rocking chair beside the ocean. An overly friendly yellow kitty purred beside me.

"A friend said he has a free table and bottles at Marquee tonight. If you're interested," I ventured to Seda.

"No thanks," Seda said. "If I'm going to get all dressed up and be hassled by drunk men, then I need to be getting paid. I can't believe girls put up with all of that crap for free."

"Some girls would probably even sleep with a guy for a free VIP table!" Daria said. We all laughed at how silly that sounds.

"You're right. I didn't want to go either. Let's stay in and get a pizza."

Unless good friends came through town on vacation, then I stayed home, or had dinner and watched a movie with friends. I'd meet up with people to listen to music and do yoga, but it was nearly impossible to get me to a party. Whenever I wasn't working, I was writing, practicing improv, or teaching yoga.

My final months in Las Vegas, I stopped living as though I was on vacation. I started to save for my next life where money wouldn't come as easily. I've never had money, but I've always been happy. I wasn't worried about luxury lost. I set a reasonable but ambitious goal for the money I needed to save from stripping in Las Vegas, and I stuck with my goal, and then I reached it, and then I passed it, and I eventually had enough money to get my next life started without too much stress.

With money in the bank, two years of yoga instructing experience, and some amazing stories written into a book called *The Yoga Stripper*, I packed up my few possessions. Happily, and sadly, I hopped in the same beat up car that had taken me across the country, from Ohio to Las Vegas, two years prior, and drove away from my Sin City home.

**

My last night dancing, I told a bouncer I wasn't getting many VIP dances.

"Don't worry about that," he said. "Look at those hips. That's pure power. I'm telling you, those hips are all power."

Damn straight.

THANK YOU

To my family for loving me so very much (even when I run away to become a Las Vegas stripper). To Ravi Krishnaney for helping me with the edits. To Lana Hines Strong for doing the final edits super quickly (you're amazing). To David Seymour for giving fantastic input and for coming up with the title by writing "Yoga/Stripper" at the top of the first draft. To Rin Hong for agreeing to appear on my original cover with me, even though she's never stripped a day in her life. To Ashley Ellwood Photography for encouraging me to create a new cover, taking the cover photograph, and for collaborating on the cover design. To http://www.chrisforephotography.com for providing the headshot for the back cover and for changing the background of the print edition from plain white to the amazingly cool looking final cover design. To Rocky Branch for the Grand Canyon, o pato, and so much more. To all of the men whose names I actually remembered, and to all of the men whose names I happily forgot. To Lisa Olson, Hannah Topangah, and Emily Jillette for loving me and letting me be a part of their wonderful lives. To all of my friends who made Vegas such an amazing experience (whether you lived with me there or simply joined me for the vacation). To the Spearmint Rhino for making me loads of money and showing me a great time. To Movie Night, my yoga classes, my Frog Lotus Yoga International training group, and my friends from improv.

And, as always, to Jim.

THANK YOU

www.theyogastripper.com/

Made in the USA
Las Vegas, NV
02 April 2023

70035945R00109